Five Lives at Harvard

Five Liv

*at Harvard: **Personality Change During College***

Stanley H. King

Harvard University Press   Cambridge, Massachusetts   1973

Preface

The preceding decade has witnessed some dramatic alterations
in behavior by college students and by adolescents and young adults
in general. Accompanying this has been a conflict between the older
and younger generations that at times has been bitter, often making
it difficult for meaningful dialogue to take place. As a result there
has been some confusion about the personality development of
young people in the late sixties. Some spokesmen for both generations have maintained that there was a unique quality in the personal
growth of that generation of adolescents that could not be accounted
for in our conventional theoretical framework of adolescent development. Thus, some older people reasoned that they could not be
expected to understand youth, and youth sometimes used the same
argument in the service of rebellion. The basic assumption of this
book, however, is that the major developmental issues in the
adolescent phase of the life cycle have changed but little. The form
the issues have taken in the last decade may be different, but the
underlying psychological processes are comparable to those observed
by psychologists and psychiatrists in previous years. Continued close
interaction with students in the classroom and consulting room for
the last fifteen years has convinced me of the consistency of developmental features in spite of changes in the social environment. The
factors that emerged from the study of students in the early sixties
strike me with the same truth as they did then.

One of the major purposes in writing this book is to clarify and

illustrate by case histories some of the patterns of normal personality development during the college years and to highlight the
coping behavior of the individuals involved. From the time this
study first began, there has been an increasing emphasis in research
on the normal person and on the derivation of theory from data
gathered in such research. This trend has come about in part because
of the deficiencies in developmental theories based on material from
patients. The idea of coping and adaptation grew on us as we
analyzed the cases reported in this book, and it was supported by
reports in the literature from other investigators. Our data and
conclusions will be useful, we hope, in broadening the base of
psychological theory.

The book evolved out of many hours of discussion between the
author and Drs. Helen H. Tartakoff and M. Robert Gardner, two
other staff members of the Harvard Student Study. The three of us
read interview material, formulated ideas about individual cases, and
then discussed concepts that tied the material together. Drafts of the
manuscript were also discussed until we arrived at some consensus
about the material. I owe to Drs. Tartakoff and Gardner a real debt
for their patience and support, and especially for their insight.

The Harvard Student Study would not have been possible without
the planning and encouragement of a number of people. Initially,
the project grew out of discussions between Dr. Leonard Duhl at the
National Institute of Mental Health and Dr. Dana L. Farnsworth,
the Director of the University Health Services. They, along with
Dr. Daniel H. Funkenstein of the Health Services, saw the project
launched and engaged my services as the director. Their support was
ever present. Dr. Farnsworth was particularly close to the Harvard
Student Study and was a constant source of support and encouragement. To him I owe special thanks.

The planning and conduct of the Harvard Student Study involved
the work of a number of people and, directly or indirectly, that work
is reflected in this book. Dr. Charles E. Bidwell conducted three of
the interviews in the freshman year and was instrumental in con-
tacting the subjects for the case history study. Subsequently he read
a draft of the manuscript and offered many thoughtful comments.
Dr. Charles C. McArthur administered the projective tests and
provided the author with superb Rorschach interpretations of the

five cases in the book. Drs. Harry Scarr and Bruce Finnie were responsible for the gathering of data from tests and questionnaires and for the analysis of those data. Dr. Finnie summarized the statistical results and thus provided supporting data for many of the conclusions reached in the clinical interviews. Dr. Rebecca S. Vreeland made a careful study of the structure and functioning of the residential Houses that was most helpful in understanding the context of personality change.

These colleagues provided an exciting intellectual climate in which to work, a climate that was made more enjoyable by the close personal relationships that we enjoyed. Working with them has filled a significant decade in my professional career.

A large research project cannot function smoothly without a capable executive secretary, and we counted ourselves lucky to have Miss Elizabeth Keul. We are grateful to her, and to a dedicated staff of typists, coders, keypunchers, and research assistants. I would like to thank Mrs. May White for her help in typing the manuscript.

A special word is in order for all the students who were willing to be subjects in the Harvard Student Study. They were patient with all our demands and invariably willing to be candid about many sectors of their private selves. I am especially grateful to the students who participated in the case history study and count it a privilege that they were willing to share so much of their lives with us. In the truest sense, we could not have done the study, nor could this book have been written, without them.

The Harvard Student Study was made possible by Grant #MH-09151 from the National Institute of Mental Health. I acknowledge that support with sincere gratitude and would like to note that emotional support and encouragement from Dr. Duhl was freely given and appreciated. The Grant Foundation provided a publication subsidy for the book, and that generosity I would also like to acknowledge with appreciation.

Stanley H. King
March 8, 1973

Contents

Five Lives at Harvard

Chapter 1 / Introduction

There are five case histories in this book, describing the lives of some college students who attended Harvard in the early sixties. Although these people are not especially unique, they struck us intuitively as representative of different types of students at Harvard at that time. What happened to them in college illustrates conclusions that we have come to about some of the developmental issues of the period in the life cycle between adolescence and full adulthood. These five young men were part of the Harvard Student Study, an extensive project that involved more than six hundred students from two Harvard classes. Thus, their histories and the conclusions that they illustrate are set in a wider context of knowledge about personality change.

These studies also came at a time when there was growing interest in assessing the impact of the college experience on young adults and in understanding the developmental tasks of that age group. Interest by behavioral scientists in such research actually began some years earlier with Theodore Newcomb's[1] pioneering study of students at Bennington College in the late 1930's. That is still a classic, and for some years was the only significant study. Some twenty years later,

1. Theodore M. Newcomb, *Personality and Social Change* (New York: Dryden Press, 1943). The reader may also be interested in a study of the same students twenty-five years later. See Theodore M. Newcomb, Kathryn E. Koenig, Richard Flacks, and Donald P. Warwick, *Persistence and Change* (New York: John Wiley and Sons, 1967).

1

Philip Jacob[2] reviewed the literature concerning the effect of the college experience on values, and subsequently a number of studies at different colleges and universities were carried out. This upsurge in research interest was aided in no small part by the availability of research grants, especially from the federal government. Projects were conducted at Vassar, the University of Michigan, Haverford, Reed, Swarthmore, Antioch, San Francisco State, Stanford, and the University of California at Berkeley, to name some of the more familiar ones. The study of Stanford and Berkeley students, as reported by Joseph Katz and his associates, and the two books by Douglas Heath on Haverford students are perhaps three of the best examples of the accumulating knowledge about personality change in college.[3] The studies reported here are in that tradition.

This book, however, differs from most books about personality change during college from other reports of the Harvard Student Study in its use of clinical evaluation and the case history method. Because of the importance for what follows, some comments about the clinical method are in order at this early point.

The word *clinical* implies the consulting room and hence an interest in illness and psychopathology. But the point of view and the method of the clinician can be applied to healthy research subjects as well as to patients. The clinical approach involves a way of looking at events that might be called naturalistic, that is, studying things as they unfold naturally. It relies more on observation than on data from tests, although the latter do provide useful information for the clinician. The approach emphasizes the total functioning of an individual in a social setting rather than discrete behaviors or characteristics.

To be more specific, the clinical method addresses itself to *dynamic process* in the individual; to the ever-changing balance between thoughts, feelings, and actions, and to the ever-changing balance between inner psychological processes and environmental forces. In studying dynamic process, consideration is given to the

2. Philip E. Jacob, *Changing Values in College* (New Haven: Edward W. Hazen Foundation, 1956).

3. Joseph Katz and Associates, *No Time for Youth* (San Francisco: Jossey-Bass, 1968); Douglas H. Heath, *Explorations of Maturity* (New York: Appleton-Century-Crofts, 1965), and *Growing Up in College* (San Francisco: Jossey-Bass, 1968).

feelings and thoughts of which the person is aware, as well as to those which for one reason or another may not be accessible to his consciousness. The clinical method attempts to assess the balance of these forces at a given point in time.

But a *temporal aspect* is also involved, for the clinical method assesses the influence of past experiences on present behavior and attempts to predict what will happen in the future, given certain conditions. As new behavior is observed, the clinician can check the hypotheses he has formed about his subject, based on information about behavior in the past.

This method can be applied to the understanding of symptoms and to their alleviation, but the method need not be limited to illness. It can be as useful in understanding the quiet and often undramatic processes of coping and adaptation. We used the method in studying a sample of the total group of students who participated in the Harvard Student Study and base the material in this book on our experiences.

There are also some other factors that should be shared with the reader, because they shape the nature of what is to follow. These are the theoretical or cognitive "set" that guided our work, the nature of the data, and the kinds of techniques used for gathering and analysing observations.

Theoretical "Set"

Several components of the cognitive framework we used come from the theoretical and empirical work of others. First, we have drawn upon psychoanalytic theory, both in the way the interviews were conducted, especially the topics covered, and in the way we organized our thinking about the data. Sigmund Freud's exposition of ego psychology is, of course, the main basis. In addition, there are the elaborations and modifications of the theory by subsequent authors, particularly by Heinz Hartmann,[4] who has spelled out in greatest detail the adaptive aspects of ego psychology. In our conclusions about personality development in college, we have been sensitive to the increase in ability or capacity to adapt and have dif-

4. Heinz Hartmann, *Ego Psychology and the Problem of Adaptation* (New York: International Universities Press, 1958).

ferentiated the term *adaptation* from the way it is used in sensory physiology, biology, or experimental psychology.

Other psychoanalytic writers have made particular contributions to aspects of adaptation. Erik Erickson's[5] scheme of the psychodynamic tasks that are posed for each individual at particular stages in his personality development has been useful in understanding not only early development, but also that of adolescence and early adulthood. The forming of a sense of ego identity was a task many of our students were still concerned with, and all of them, to some extent, worked on the task of developing intimacy with others. Erickson's ideas alerted us to potential difficulties in adaptation, such as those occasioned by the identity crisis, as well as to strategies that students might use in working out developmental tasks.

Peter Blos[6] has emphasized the reintegrative aspects of development in late adolescence and early adulthood. Following the resolution of identity tasks, or accompanying this in the later stages, there is an altered state of personal organization into which impulses must be accommodated, impulses that in themselves have been altered because of the physiological changes of adolescence. We have thus been sensitive to an awareness by our subjects of altered personality organization, particularly of a feeling of reorganization on some kind of new level.

Another theoretical and research effort has influenced our work: the studies of life histories of students, which began with the group that Henry Murray assembled in the Psychological Clinic at Harvard in the late 1930's. One of the early results of that work was *Explorations in Personality*,[7] which, among other things, presented a conceptual system of psychological needs and a corresponding or reciprocal system of presses. The needs might be considered secondary, or elaborated needs, compared with basic biological drives, but they are strong motivators for behavior, and Murray and his colleagues demonstrated how they can be assessed and used in understanding behavior over a life span. Of equal importance to the conceptual scheme were the innovations in assessment procedures,

5. Erik H. Erikson, "Identity and the Life Cycle," *Psychological Issues*, vol. 1, no. 1 (Monograph 1), 1959.
6. Peter Blos, *On Adolescence* (Glencoe, Ill.: Free Press, 1962).
7. Henry A. Murray et al., *Explorations in Personality* (New York: Oxford University Press, 1938).

most notably the Thematic Apperception Test, on which we depended for data in our own study.

One of Murray's colleagues who was important in continuing the tradition of studying lives was Robert White.[8] He also made a contribution to personality theory by his concept of competence, or the sense of efficacy, as a motivator in behavior. Competence can occur in athletic, intellectual, or interpersonal aspects of a person's life and depends not only on what others may think or say to him, but also on his own feelings of capacity or ability. White noted that college is a period of time when competence can be reinforced or extended, and even sometimes discovered by an individual.

In the work of both Murray and White there is a good deal of emphasis on the interaction between the person and his environment, Murray's need-press system being a good illustration. They have seen the individual as responsive to what goes on around him, but also as changing or molding conditions to his advantage. These ideas have seemed important to us in understanding the process of adaptation, particularly in the context of the college experience.

Several studies of students have also influenced our intellectual "set," particularly in terms of the categories of behavior they developed or the manner in which they sensitized us to features of development in the college years.

Students at George Williams College were studied by Roy Grinker,[9] who began his investigation expecting to find psychopathology and ended by finding successful adjustment. The value to us of his work was the manner in which he related early rearing practices and values of parents to personality characteristics of students, especially to the techniques they utilized in dealing with the environment and to the life style they selected. His conclusions stressed the importance of identification in personality development.

A research group at the National Institute of Mental Health, David Hamburg, Earle Silber, and George Coelho,[10] studied a group of high school students as they prepared to enter college. From a develop-

8. Robert W. White, "Motivation Reconsidered: The Concept of Competence," *Psychological Review*, 66 (September 1959), 297–333.

9. Roy R. Grinker, " 'Mentally Healthy' Young Males (Homoclites)," *Archives of General Psychiatry*, 6 (June 1962), 405–453.

10. Earle Silber et al., "Adaptive Behavior in Competent Adolescents: Coping with the Anticipation of College," *Archives of General Psychiatry*, 5 (1961), 354–365, and "Competent Adolescents Coping with College

mental point of view, their data covered a period just prior to the one that we studied, although there was some overlap. Their work was helpful through the behavioral categories of coping that came from activities of their subjects. They studied people who were successful in handling the move away from home, and thus they could describe the coping strategies used in anticipation of college entrance and assess their later success. They also studied the students' fantasy productions, using a version of the Thematic Apperception Test, as one means of predicting success in coping.

The two reports of a study of students at Haverford by Heath[11] differ from the studies just cited in that the author proposes a theory of development toward maturity and uses data to show how this takes place in college. The key elements in his scheme are growing intellectuality, forming guiding values, becoming knowledgeable about oneself, developing social and interpersonal skills, becoming able to symbolize one's experience, and becoming more allocentric, integrated, stable, and autonomous. These are not new or unusual characteristics, but Heath demonstrates how some individuals change in the direction of greater maturity or do so at a faster rate than other students. Although we have not used the concept of maturity in our case histories, we have benefited from Heath's ideas in understanding change and the adaptation process.

Effects of the Data

The characteristics of data under consideration put rough limits around the kind of conclusions that can be drawn. In our situation, certain features of our sample directed some of the broad outlines and the limitations of our findings.

Our students were drawn from a rather narrow range of the general population in terms of conventional intelligence, as inferred from scores on tests and previous academic performance. For example, the average verbal score on the Scholastic Aptitude Test was 673, the average quantitative score, 698. Many of the entering students had been valedictorians of their graduating classes in secondary schools.

Decisions," *Archives of General Psychiatry*, 5 (1961), 517–527; George V. Coelho, David A. Hamburg, and Elizabeth B. Murphy, "Coping Strategies in a New Learning Environment: A Study of American College Freshmen," *Archives of General Psychiatry*, 9 (1963), 433–443.

11. Heath, *Explorations of Maturity* and *Growing Up in College*.

By and large the students were intellectually gifted, and a few could be expected in later years to make notable contributions to knowledge or to society. They were not more intelligent, however, than their counterparts in many other colleges and universities. Nevertheless, there are limitations on the nature of the inferences that can be drawn from the data. Our subjects were not typical of all college students or of the population that did not attend college.

There is reason to believe that the selection process for admission to Harvard affected other characteristics of our sample besides intellectual competence. Most of the students had been active in some manner: active in the sense of doing something creative, like writing or building science projects; or in carrying out social activities, as in clubs, class officerships, or community projects; or in athletics. Most of the students had thus demonstrated an ability to engage the environment in varied ways. This characteristic is certainly not confined either to students entering Harvard or to men who go on to college. The admissions process, however, probably produced in our sample a higher concentration of "effective engagers" than one would find in a random sample of the population, and perhaps at many other colleges and universities.

Our subjects were different from what would have been found had they all been drawn from the consulting room. The term *mental health* is hard to define and weighted with value judgments, but most observers would likely agree that our students were "healthier" than one would find in clinical practice. This, of course, is a matter of degree; some of our subjects developed symptoms of sufficient severity so that they and others knew they needed help. Some left college for emotional reasons, and others sought psychiatric help while continuing their education. The majority, however, functioned effectively and did not report severe or prolonged psychic distress. On this characteristic they share features in common with many students at other colleges and with people their own age who do not go to college. The fact that they have demonstrated competence in dealing with the world and have continued to do so affects the material in the rest of the book.

Selection and Data-Gathering Procedures

The manner in which subjects are selected for a research project and the techniques used for obtaining information from those subjects also determine in some manner the conclusions that can be drawn.

Students were chosen initially by random number; that is, they came from a larger group that had been thus selected. More than that, each fulfilled certain characteristics that we had come to understand as identifying the types of students at Harvard. Thus, they appeared on our sample list as faceless names, but they did not stay that way for long; they became people we liked and watched over with even a certain parental interest. But first, how did their names turn up on our lists, other than through random selection?

From the class list of students coming to Harvard a 25 percent random sample was drawn. To this sample were added the top five and the bottom five names on the listing of prospective students according to predicted academic rank. Also, as far as could be determined, all American-born Blacks were included. These steps were taken to ensure the collection of data from groups for whom the college experience might be particularly meaningful or potentially stressful. Also, all students who had taken part in Project Talent were included. Together, these constituted the total research list of students from whom cooperation was sought for participation in the study.

Within this list a special selection was made of fifty students, chosen to represent a cross-section of the College. Previous experience with the College had provided us with information about the major differentiating variables among Harvard students. We wished our sample to have a few individuals in each of the groups defined by these differentiating variables. From the beginning, then, this was not a statistical subsample, but a selection based on knowledge of the college population. The manner in which major variables influenced the selection process was as follows.

1. *Secondary school background.* At the time of our study, Harvard drew about 40 to 45 percent of its entering class from private preparatory schools. Among these, three groups could be distinguished. First are what have come to be called the "St. Grottlesex" schools, a small group of older schools located in the East, usually Episcopal by affiliation, with a tradition of educating sons from upper-class families in the Eastern Establishment. The second group comprised the two largest private boarding schools, Phillips Academy (Andover) and Phillips Exeter. Both schools are well endowed and have long

been able to offer scholarships; thus their students represented a wider social class range. Both schools, in addition, have a tradition of superb secondary school teaching. For a long time they had contributed many students each year to the Harvard freshman class. The third and largest group comprised all other independent secondary schools, both in New England and in other parts of the United States. We selected a number of students from each of the three groups.

Among students who had attended public schools, we wanted a selection that would range from the most sophisticated urban school systems to rather small rural schools. Harvard drew, and still does draw, students from all parts of the United States, hence from all types of public school systems. Public school typology is determined by social demographic variables; thus our selection here was closely related to selection on other variables.

2. *Socioeconomic status.* Due to an extensive scholarship program, students from most socioeconomic strata were able to attend Harvard. We say "most" because relatively few men or women from the lower class attend college, Harvard or otherwise. Our assessment of SES was determined by father's occupation, work title, and undergraduate college attended. By using these data in connection with type of secondary school attended and home residence, we could make a relatively sophisticated distribution by social class from what would appear to be rather crude demographic data. Parenthetically, we wanted a number of students in our sample whose fathers had attended Harvard because of the social implications this had for certain aspects of undergraduate life.

3. *Race and religion.* Although historically Harvard has drawn heavily from the Protestant population, more specifically from what has been called the WASP group, this pattern has changed considerably since the Second World War. At the time of our study, we estimated that some 10 to 15 percent of the student body would come from a Roman Catholic background and around 25 percent from a Jewish background. Also, for some time Harvard had been making a determined effort to enroll qualified Black students, especially from ghetto and rural areas. According to Massachusetts law, questions about religious affiliation and racial background cannot be asked prior to admission. Selection on these variables, therefore, had to depend on name for religion and on a photograph from the health form for race. We tried to choose appropriate numbers of Catholics,

Protestants, and Jews and to have several Blacks. Subsequent experience with the sample indicated that our selection was remarkably representative.

5. *Athletics.* Competence in athletics has long been part of the Harvard tradition, in keeping with the notion of the well-rounded personality where intellectual ability and athletic prowess are combined. Harvard has not denied admission to able students because they are also good athletes. Our knowledge of the student environment indicated that the athletic subculture was a distinct part of the undergraduate scene and could be further subdivided into the more rugged contact sports like football and hockey and sports like crew, squash, and track. Alumni interviewers of prospective students have usually noted, among other skills, athletic achievements, and hence a list of potential athletes was available in advance of matriculation. We wanted some students in our sample who would be likely to participate in varsity sports as well as some who would be active in intramural, or House, sports events. Subsequent experience with our selection again indicated that our sample was very representative.

6. *Intellectual potential.* Like most colleges and universities, Harvard has hoped that some of its students will be outstanding scholars. The tradition of scholarship and intellectual elitism has been a clearly visible value among both faculty and students. Although not expected or demanded of every student, it has some pulling power on almost all students. We hoped that our sample would contain a few students who would graduate *summa cum laude* or who would write unusually good senior honors theses. We were aware of the fact that most multivariate predictors of academic success have a multiple correlation coefficient of around .55 or .60; hence we could not be very certain in advance as to who would be Phi Beta Kappa or write a *summa* thesis. By selecting some students who had high SAT scores and had demonstrated outstanding achievement in secondary school, we trusted that our net would snare one or more potential scholars. Indeed it did.

7. *Commuting status.* Although Harvard has vigorously encouraged students to "live in," a place has always been made for a small number of students from the surrounding communities who, for economic or other reasons, wished to be commuters. It is rare that a student stays a commuter for all four years; most move into the Houses by the junior year. The commuters constitute an important

group, however, because they maintain ties to the home community while pursuing their studies. This group, therefore, was represented in our sample.

These selection variables were based on what we knew about Harvard before we drew a study sample. Before proceeding further with a description of the design of the life history investigation, we should give a brief account of the demographic characteristics of the total random sample, to provide a fuller context for the data presented in succeeding chapters.

The majority of fathers were in professional or managerial positions. A small percentage were owner-managers of their own firms or salesmen, and only 5 percent were unskilled workers. Thirty percent of the fathers and 56 percent of the mothers did not graduate from college. Approximately 20 percent of fathers and of mothers attended a private secondary school. As of 1961–1962, when our data on background factors were gathered, 37 percent of the families had incomes under $10,000 and 26 percent had incomes over $20,000. Political affiliation showed an equal division; 37 percent of fathers and mothers called themselves Republicans and an equal number called themselves Democrats. Fifty-four percent of our sample came from Protestant families, 10 percent from Roman Catholic, 24 percent from Jewish, and the rest from mixed backgrounds. It is of more than passing interest that 86 percent of our sample came from families where both parents were alive and living together and only 5 percent from families where there was a divorce or separation. People interested in birth order will note that 60 percent of our sample were either first or only children. Sixty percent came from public school and 26 percent of the total sample were first in their graduating class in secondary school; first in their families and first in their schools.

Now to return to our fifty students. We contacted each in person after the academic year had begun, explained the goals and procedures of the project, indicated what would be required of him, and asked if he would be willing to participate. One subject was lost to us even before we were able to contact him; he had to leave college temporarily for pressing personal reasons. The other forty-nine agreed to take part and were offered a modest honorarium for their efforts. We also assured the students of confidentiality of information. In this we had excellent cooperation from the Dean of the

College; he agreed that even the names of participants should not be known to him, and they never have been revealed to anyone outside the project staff. Transmission of material from the study files to any other person has been done only at the direct request of the subject and with his written permission, and then only for medical reasons.

Forty students completed all the testing and interviewing. Among those we lost, one dropped out of Harvard after his freshman year to attend another college, one completed so little of his freshman test and questionnaire material that he was dropped from the research, and another completed little of his material and in addition was asked to leave Harvard for a poor academic record. Four students decided by the end of the sophomore year that they no longer wanted to participate. We felt at the time that they resented our efforts as an invasion of privacy; they exercised an option that had been open to them from the beginning. Another student left Harvard because of emotional difficulties, and although we had fragmentary contact with him later, we did not have sufficient data to keep him in the project. Finally, one student dropped out of Harvard and eventually finished at another university. With him we were able to keep in close touch and to continue the testing and most of the interviewing. In this interview group our completion rate was thus 80 percent, quite a respectable figure when compared to most longitudinal studies.

Each subject in the case history sample filled out the same "paper and pencil" tests and questionnaires as did the subjects in the larger survey sample. In addition, each case history student was interviewed and given certain individually administered projective tests. The scheduling and content of these procedures is detailed below.

Freshman year

Three social history interviews were conducted by Charles E. Bidwell—near the time of the first hour exam, after Christmas vacation, and at the end of the year. The emphasis was on activities, interests, appraisal of teachers, reaction to courses, division of time, characteristics of peer group, and perception of the values and norms of Harvard. During the fall, the present author carried out a family history interview with emphasis on family structure and relations, developmental history of the student, early memories, significant experience outside the family, and other important previous life experiences. In the spring, he also had a "Harvard Day" interview, in which the student was asked to describe in great detail one of his days at Harvard (not necessarily a typical day). He was asked to describe his feelings about people and events as well as activity. During the winter, Phyllis Courtney interviewed each student about career goals and plans, seeking the reasons for career choice, if one or several were in mind, or reasons for rejecting certain career lines, if this had been done. Both the Rorschach Inkblot Test and the Thematic Apperception Test (T.A.T.) were administered by Charles C. McArthur, the former in the autumn and the latter during the spring term.

Sophomore year

An interview in the fall was conducted by King to find out about summer experiences, relationships with parents and others in the family, reactions to the beginning of the second year at Harvard, and plans for the year. All subsequent interviews were done by him. During the winter another "Harvard Day" interview was held, and toward the end of the spring each student was interviewed in order to assess the year. He was questioned about his reaction to courses and other events at Harvard, his peer-group relationships during the year, his feelings about himself and about important issues of the day, and his plans for the summer. Also, a second Rorschach was administered by McArthur.

Junior year

The interview schedule paralleled that for the sophomore year, and no projective tests were given.

Senior year

Only two interviews were held, one in the fall and one in the spring. In the latter the student was asked to assess his experience at Harvard in addition to his reaction to the senior year. He was also asked to look ahead and outline his occupational plans as well as his life goals. McArthur administered a third Rorschach and a second T.A.T.

All interviews were tape recorded and later converted to typescript. This material provides the basic information for the conclusions presented in the subsequent chapters.

We are aware of at least two problems in utilizing our interview data. The first is one of validity. Were our subjects candid? Did they tell us how they really felt, or did they report information they thought was safe or was what we wanted to hear? Definitive answers to these questions are not forthcoming, because standards against which to assess validity are not readily available. We can only cite secondary information. First, the completion rate was higher for subjects in the case history group than in the survey group. The students appeared to enjoy the interviews and to be committed to the project. They talked about very personal matters with openness and frankness. Many said that we knew them better than their parents or anyone else did. Also there was a noticeable consistency to what they said over the four years. We are inclined to accept the evidence from the interviews as valid but are cognizant of its potential shortcomings.

A different problem concerns the effect of the interviewing process on personality change. An opportunity to talk about oneself, about goals, values, future plans, and, most importantly, about fears, disappointments, and conflicts, would have an organizing and synthesizing effect on the personality over four years. Even though the interviewer was quite objective and noninvolved, interaction with him may have had therapeutic value. If these effects were true, a bias would be introduced into the data that would have to be considered in interpreting results.

An answer to this problem is not easy to obtain. Changes resulting from the interviewing process might be subtle, even though important, and difficult to pick up except by an investigative process that in itself might produce change. At any rate, an ideal research design to control for the problem would involve selecting matched control subjects, who had many characteristics in common with the research subjects and who might be expected to react in the college experience in much the same way. We do not yet know all the significant variables on which to match controls, and thus such a design is ideal rather than practical. Another technique for answering the problem would be to compare the group of subjects in the case history sample with those in the survey sample, who were given only "paper and pencil" tests. This we have done.

In another part of the Harvard Student Study, data from the battery of tests and questionnaires were analyzed by subjecting them to a factor analysis. A large quantity of variables were thus reduced to a manageable number, and change scores could be calculated by subtracting the freshman factor score from the senior factor score. Statistical significance was determined by summing the differences for the entire group of subjects on a given factor, deriving a mean difference and comparing it with zero by a "t" test. In order to compare the case history sample with the rest of the survey sample, mean differences were computed on each factor for each group and "t" tests were calculated.

Perhaps of most importance was the fact that on no factor did the two groups show mean differences in the opposite direction at a statistically significant level. At the same time, there were 43 factors out of 194 where both groups changed in the same direction at a statistically significant level. There were a number of factors, 51, where the difference for one group was statistically significant, but for the other group the difference was above the .05 probability level. In almost all of these instances it was the survey group that showed significant change. In some cases, this was due to properties of the statistical tests; that is, with larger numbers in a group, it may be easier to achieve a significant probability level, even though the difference being tested may actually be smaller. The survey group had almost four times as many students as the case history group.

However, a number of factors remained where the difference for the survey group was larger than for the case history group, as well as statistically significant. The general picture that emerges from those differences is one of *greater sociability* (active "going out," letter-writing to friends, number of friends, and desire for sociability), *greater independence* (amount of own income, amount of income-producing work during the school year, and decrease in letter-writing to family), *higher expectations of and desire for large income from future job,* and *lower feelings of inadequacy.* One of the few factors where the difference was significant for the case history group alone was *preference for a bureaucratic type of job.*

What may we conclude from these results? First, the two groups were very much alike in the areas and extent of change between freshman and senior years. The survey group, however, did move toward greater sociability and independence and desire for greater income. If these differences between the survey and case history groups could be ascribed to the interviews, it would suggest that the interviews had an inhibiting rather than a releasing effect. Other factors could have intervened, of course, and we have no way of knowing if that was so. We are inclined to believe that the effect of the interviews was minimal and that the data from them reflect what was actually going on in the subjects' lives.

Before we move into the main body of this book another small digression is in order. The reader who is not familiar with Harvard College may find useful a brief summary of the structure and culture of the College in the early part of the last decade, especially as that structure affected undergraduates.

The College is centered in the Yard, the site of the original buildings, an area that impinges on Harvard Square on two sides and is surrounded by wall or fence. In the Yard are the administration buildings, the main library, Memorial Church, some of the classroom buildings, and the majority of the freshman dormitories. Thus, when we did our study, freshmen lived apart from other students and took their meals in the Freshman Union. The next three years were spent in one of the eight Houses along the Charles River. Only a few students commuted.

The Houses are unique in a number of ways, of which one noteworthy aspect is the "entry system." There are a number of stairwells in each House, with entrances to two or three suites of rooms on each floor of the stairwell. Each suite has a living room, one or more bedrooms, and a bathroom; suites can accommodate from two to five persons. The effect is more akin to an apartment building than to the traditional long-corridor arrangement of most college housing in the United States. Each House has its own dining room, library, junior common room, and in some cases a darkroom, squash courts, swimming pool, or other amenities. A number of graduate student tutors live in each House; a House Master, usually a senior faculty member, has a residence there, as does a Senior Tutor, and a number of faculty members in the University have affiliation with the House as Associates. The Houses were designed to be centers for social and intellectual interchange and often did serve that purpose for our students, and for many students they also helped to reduce Harvard to manageable size.

When our study was conducted there were rules limiting the hours during which women could be entertained in student rooms, and jackets and ties were mandatory at all meals in the dining room. In both areas the rules no longer exist.

The Radcliffe dormitories were located "on the other side of the Yard," and although classes were coeducational there was a feeling of separateness between the two institutions. Although Harvard students did date Radcliffe women, they also went to Wellesley and other "Seven Sister" colleges.

Academic life at Harvard showed an interesting mixture of elements. On the one hand, a student could go through four years without doing a great deal of studying and yet graduate with passing grades. Perhaps this was a result of the tradition of the "gentleman's C," which still had an effect on academic life. At the same time, superior performance was highly rewarded and reflected the notion that bright students shared a kind of colleagueship with their instructors. There was a wide range of courses from which a student could pick and choose, and rules relating to studies offered considerable latitude for an imaginative and resourceful student. There was no doubt, however, that academic excellence was the underlying theme, even though students were not discriminated against if they chose not to, or could not attain it.

Finally, a factor should be mentioned that will be emphasized a number of times later on, that is, that there was no single honorific status among students. No single constellation of factors defined the "big man on campus" syndrome. Rather, the Harvard culture emphasized individuality and gave prestige to varied types of accomplishments—athletic, artistic, intellectual, and organizational.

Finally, here is a brief outline of what is to come. Chapters two and four present an outline of the factors that guided us as we pondered the data and were substantiated by what we observed. In a sense, we approached our cases with certain assumptions about personality, which we tested and revised as we went along. It would be quite unfair to claim that the study was one of hypothesis-testing; it was more that of hypothesis-generating or hypothesis-evolving. In the course of the analysis we became particularly interested in certain of the students and selected five of them for a full presentation here. They are not pure cases in the sense of illustrating most clearly our conclusions, but their experiences do represent, if imperfectly, some of the ways in which students in our project changed. Following the case presentations, there is in the final chapter a summary of our experience.

Chapter 2 / *Adaptation and Growth*

Our subjects began college as late adolescents and graduated as young adults. That interval of time is not well understood in terms of the major personality growth tasks that are fulfilled then; the literature on earlier stages of development is voluminous by comparison. College students have not been ignored as objects of study; quite the contrary, no population has come under scrutiny as detailed, especially in psychology classes. But much of the research has been fragmented, has considered only single or very limited variables, and has taken measurements at only one point in time. Few studies have looked upon these four years as a life phase, like latency or adolescence, in which important developmental changes might take place.

To complicate matters, many of the ideas and theories that do exist about these years come from investigators who have drawn their data primarily from the consulting room. They have had the advantage of observing development in all its complexity, and have followed it over time, but the development they have followed has often been painful and disrupted in some respects. Hence, their conclusions may not accurately reflect the way that growth tasks are handled by college students, and others of that age, who do not have emotional difficulties.

Our perspective, then, must be a broad one, taking into consideration the whole four-year period, the interaction of a number of variables, and realizing that important changes may be hard to see because they are subtle and quiet. Our task is to describe and document a few of the changes that appear to be unique to this life phase.

Our subjects also began college as the decade of the sixties was coming in. The succeeding years have witnessed some striking changes in the youth culture and life style and in the behavior of some college students, alterations in college policies and curricula, and growing ferment in society in general. Our subjects graduated just as the wave of interest in and use of psychoactive drugs was forming and as student activism in universities was becoming established. Harvard is a place where all these changes have been quite evident, hence a place where social expectations and pressures on students were different at the end of the decade than they were at the beginning. We are not unmindful of the fact that our conceptualization of growth tasks must be broad enough so that personality development can be understood equally well under varying social conditions. One eye has had to be on the students that we studied and one on those who have come to college subsequently.

Adaptation

The most general approach to describing and interpreting our data is based on the dynamic balance between each student and his environment, with special emphasis on the college environment. To find a specific term, or terms, for the processes involved is not easy. In many ways *adaptation* is best, even though it has several meanings within the scientific community.

Its basic meaning is to fit, suit, or adjust, and biologists use it to mean adjustment to conditions in order to survive, modification of organic systems or responses to fit a plant or animal more perfectly for environmental conditions. In this sense, *adaptation* has been used to cover a range of behaviors, from simple sensorimotor response patterns within the organism to the alteration of social behavior within groups of animals, especially human groups. Changes in social behavior for adaptation often represent very complex patterns of interaction. The end result of adaptation, if successful, is a tendency toward a steady state or homeostasis within the organism or group.

The emphasis in the biological use of the term *adaptation* is on modification within the organism or group, with little or no emphasis on efforts by the organism to alter the environment to suit the organism's characteristics. There is also nothing in the definition to suggest that on occasion the organism may put itself in a situation away from a steady state, as if there were pleasure to be gained through efforts at altering conditions back toward a steady state. Sometimes humans create problems with their environment seemingly for the sheer joy of solving them.

Adaptation has a more limited meaning in sensory physiology, where it refers to a decline in intensity of sensation or of muscular response as a result of continued and regular stimulation or of continued response. There are initial rapid changes in receptor organs, then a slower change, leading to a plateau state of the rate of discharge in the receptors. Dark adaptation in the eye would be a familiar illustration.

Of more recent use in psychology is the concept of *adaptation level*. It is based on the premise that adaptation is affected by the reaction of the person to stimulation as well as by the action of stimulation on the organism. Important to the concept is the determination of equilibrium states, which serve as reference points. But because of the changing nature of processes in the organism, responses denoting equilibrium states change. In Harry Helson's[1] definition, there is in every situation confronting the organism an adaptation level, or internal standard, or baseline, which is the result of present stimuli, their background, and past experience. Adaptation level is the weighted mean of these stimuli. New stimuli do not have constant effects on the organism but reflect instead a relationship between stimulation and the current norm or equilibrium state. Adaptation level is not only relevant to traditional sensory phenomena; Helson sees its utility in social behavior as well.

There is another meaning of *adaptation*, as used in ego psychology, and that is the form to be followed here. As a background for this usage, it is important to remember that man differs from other animals in at least two respects: in the extent of his intelligence and his ability to use symbols, and in the temporal quality of his consciousness, where past and future enter into responses to the environment along with the present. Because of man's abilities, he has

1. Harry Helson, *Adaptation Level Theory* (New York: Harper and Row, 1964).

created a complex social environment, which raises special problems of adaptation. Also, because of his abilities, he is able to respond to, rather than react to, the environment, and to respond in ways that can enhance particular and idiosyncratic needs and wishes. René Dubos puts this very well:

> The biological view of adaptation is inadequate for human life because neither survival of the body, nor of the species, nor fitness to the conditions of the present, suffices to encompass the richness of man's nature. The uniqueness of man comes from the fact that he does not live only in the present; he still carries the past in his body and in his mind, and he is concerned with the future. To be really relevant to the human condition, the concept of adaptability must incorporate not only the needs of the present, but also the limitations imposed by the past, and the anticipations of the future.[2]

And in another place:

> But experience shows that human beings are not passive components in adaptive systems. Their responses commonly manifest themselves as acts of personal creation. Each individual person tries to achieve some self-selected end even while he is responding to stimuli and adapting to them.[3]

Now as to a more precise definition—*adaptation* is used in ego psychology by George Rosenwald to describe "the encounter and mutual transformation of person and outer reality."[4] *A Glossary of Psychoanalytic Terms and Concepts* gives the following definition: "Adaptation involves the capacity to cope reasonably, yet advantageously, with the environment. While it requires conformity to the *reality* of the external world, it does not preclude activity directed toward its change. The term may refer to either the state of adaptedness which obtains between the organism and his

2. René Dubos, *Man Adapting* (New Haven: Yale University Press, 1965), p. 279.
3. Ibid., p. 18.
4. George C. Rosenwald, "Personality Description from the Viewpoint of Adaptation," *Psychiatry*, 31 (1968), 18.

environment, or the process of adaptation which brings about that state."[5]

The ego is the main instrument of adaptation, dealing with id drives, superego dictates, and the particular characteristics and demands of reality outside the person. Adaptation can proceed more easily when the ego is relatively autonomous from drives, superego, and reality; autonomy allows for "greater range of choices in adaptive responses in problem-solving and in decision-making, and in the development of the means of obtaining pleasure, gratification and well-being."[6] With autonomy there is freedom to explore new solutions to problems posed by reality without disruption of the internal feeling state of well-being.

Particular behaviors or personality characteristics are not adaptive or maladaptive per se but are adaptive in some respects or situations and not others. Also, as life situations change, some behaviors may no longer be adaptive, though once they were.

The key aspects of this use of the term *adaptation*, then, are action by the ego, the organism's personal needs and wishes, and the possibility of choosing courses of behavioral interaction. Adaptation is a process, a dynamic feedback between organism and environment, wherein both organism and environment may be transformed or changed. The end or steady state toward which the ego strives in the process of adaptation is gratification and pleasure.

A distinction can and should be made between *adaptation* and other terms similar in nature. Thus, we distinguish *adaptation* from *adjustment*, which means a bringing into correspondence of the person and the environment; likewise, from *accomodating* or *conforming*, which mean a yielding, or giving in to the demands of the environment. At times, of course, the process of adaptation may involve adjusting or conforming to situations in which the person finds himself, if those behaviors are in the service of ego activity that is active and creative. Jeanne Lampl–De Groot makes the

5. Burgess E. Moore and Bernard D. Fine (eds.), *A Glossary of Psychoanalytic Terms and Concepts* (New York: American Psychoanalytic Association, 1968), p. 5.

6. W. G. Joffe and Joseph Sandler, "Comments on the Psychoanalytic Psychology of Adaptation, with Special Reference to the Role of Affects and the Representational World," *International Journal of Psycho-analysis,* 49 (1968), 445–454.

distinction by saying that conforming behavior involves a passive surrender to internal or external pressures and to anxiety, whereas adaptation is "behavior directed by a creative assessment of inner and outer factors and leading to equilibrium and constructive action."[7]

When regarded intrapsychically, adaptation can be characterized in terms of *efficiency*; from the point of view of the environment, the reference is *effectiveness*. The first of these terms describes the degree to which various parts of the personality system function smoothly together. We speak of balance among motivating factors— needs, drives, and goals; directional factors—beliefs, attitudes, and values; skill factors—cognitive ability and coordination; and appraisal and control factors—self-concept, conscience, and defense and coping mechanisms. Efficiency comes when the ego can mediate these factors without tying up excessive emotional energy in intrapsychic conflict or the control of guilt and anxiety, leaving the person freer for selecting alternative ways of dealing with the environment. The internal aspect of the adaptation process is *autoplastic*—that is, the formative or creative functioning which is directed toward the self.

Effectiveness describes the degree to which the person is able to become actively engaged with the environment, to adjust to various environmental demands, and to alter the environment to meet his personal needs and wishes without disrupting or causing excessive conflict in his physical and social surroundings. Here is the *alloplastic* aspect of adaptation: formative or creative functioning directed toward the environment.

Because adaptation involves an interaction process, we must consider the fact that behavior can be efficient as far as an individual is concerned but ineffective from the social point of view. Thus, a person might be disruptive of group activity or, in contrast, might not become involved or might even withdraw from social activity, yet have little internal tension and considerable stability. The converse can also be true; effective social behavior may occur at the cost of great inner pain and conflict. The most adaptive behavior is both efficient and effective. Said differently, adaptation is the

7. Jeanne Lampl-De Groot, "Some Thoughts on Adaptation and Conformism," in Rudolph M. Lowenstein et al., (eds.), *Psychoanalysis: A General Psychology* (New York: International Universities Press, 1966), pp. 347–348.

capacity to integrate skills, needs, and defenses with pressures and conditions of the environment, all at a special point in time and in a special environmental setting with certain opportunities.

To the extent that the ego can exercise control in the process of adaptation, we can speak of *adaptive capacity*, a term that has a future or predictive orientation. By observing the encounters between a person and environments, we gain an idea of what may happen in new situations when there are altered internal or environmental conditions. If there is the possibility of choice of actions by the ego, then some individuals are more likely than others to be efficient and/or effective in new adaptations. Judgment about that is a judgment of capacity.

The nature of the environment is important in adaptation, not only in the pressures it exerts on the person, but also in the allowances it makes for different kinds of adaptive responses. In some situations there may be a range of possibilities, that is, of behaviors by the person that would suit the conditions, or there may be enough flexibility for a person to make trial adaptations in the feedback process without incurring penalty. Some environments may subtly or directly encourage trial adaptations. Four years in a liberal arts college may offer a greater range of choices for the individual than four years in the army, or, to put it differently, there may be a greater number of ways in which a person can adapt effectively in a college than in the army.

Finally, we return to temporal factors in adaptation, but speak of them now in a slightly different way. There is a difference between that adaptive behavior relative to the immediate present and that considered from long-term perspective. What is adaptive now may militate against adaptation in the future; the reverse, of course, is equally true. Colloquial expressions have captured this dilemma quite colorfully: "We lost the battle but won the war," or "The operation was successful, but the patient died."

Changes in the physical or social situation facing the person or group affect the temporal aspects of adaptation. The industrial development of the world in the last few decades has been rapid, and some small and isolated countries have had a difficult time with the ensuing social changes. A style of life that was adaptive for an ordered, tightly knit, agricultural society is quite inappropriate for a social situation that uses many labor-saving devices, empha-

sizes production, and rewards relationships based on economic factors rather than lineal ones. Social participation and expectations vary from one life phase to another, sometimes making earlier behavior incongruent with later requirements. A college student may go along with the crowd, enter into an active extracurricular life, and adapt to the collegiate ethic, yet subsequently find that he is ill prepared for pursuing graduate training in a professional school that challenges his basic intellectual ability.

In our study of lives, we had an opportunity to observe adaptation over a four-year period and thus could make some judgments about its success. We came to two major conclusions. First, some individuals seem to have an *adaptive sense*, when we consider a time span, seem to know where they are going and how behavior at one life phase will mesh with behavior at a later life phase. In caricature, the obsessive-compulsive personality fits this picture because he "overplans" as a defense against the threat of mistakes. At the other extreme is the impulse-ridden personality, who gives little thought to the future and even ignores many qualities of the present. In contrast to these poles, a person with a good adaptive sense has a certain shrewdness about the impact events will have on him and how he will change in the future. Although some people have this ability from early years, many learn it as part of their development. We feel that this is a specific outcome of the college years and one of the major growth tasks.

The second point is akin to the first: our students showed more instances of successful adaptation as they progressed from freshman to senior year. Perhaps this follows so closely from our first point as to appear redundant, but there is a subtle difference. When a problem of living was presented, the students were more able by senior year to organize their personality resources to meet it, not simply to adjust to it but to adapt to it in a creative manner, often altering aspects of the environment to make it more acceptable. We would hardly expect their adaptive ability to stop in its development after college, but we feel the spurt in success in adaptation is a signal quality of this life phase.

Models of Personality Development

How does increasing ability to adapt come about? There are two different ways of regarding the process of development in adolescence and young adulthood, or what we might call two different conceptual models of growth. The model frequently espoused, especially in the clinical literature, can be referred to as the *crisis model*, or what Daniel Offer[8] calls the psychiatric approach. The model that will be presented in our study can be referred to as the *continuity model*. These two approaches are not necessarily antithetical, but adherence to one or the other can affect the manner in which one interprets and predicts behavior.

The crisis model emphasizes that significant growth occurs more frequently when there is a period of disruption and turmoil, followed eventually by a reintegration of personality in a somewhat altered form. This approach implies that if conflict and crisis do not take place in adolescence, then development will in some way be impaired and emotional maturity will be reached only with difficulty in later years.

There are a number of sources of support for the crisis model; one is the psychiatric, and especially the psychoanalytic, literature. Anna Freud,[9] for example, has referred to adolescence as a "developmental disturbance." One of the main tasks of the adolescent, in her view, is to find ways of handling the increase in aggressive and sexual drives that come with puberty and in the process to find new ways of relating to parents and peers. She does not feel that the ego is strong enough at this time to handle the increased drives in an integrated, harmonious way; hence, the task cannot be accomplished without upheaval in personality functioning.

Another psychoanalytic writer, Erikson,[10] has described the major growth task of adolescence and young adulthood as the establishment of a stable identity. For many young people this may involve questioning of one's values, of one's place in the world of work, and establishing a unique sense of selfhood that is different from parents and other authority figures. In so doing, conflict with parents can result, and rebellion can be strong and bitter. The breaking away often involves actions that lead to anger on both sides

8. Daniel Offer, *The Psychological World of the Teen-Ager* (New York: Basic Books, 1969).

9. Anna Freud, "Adolescence as a Developmental Disturbance," in Gerald Caplan and Serge Lebovici (eds.), *Adolescence: Psychosocial Perspectives* (New York: Basic Books, 1969), pp. 5–10.

10. Erik H. Erikson, "Identity and the Life Cycle," *Psychological Issues,* vol. 1, no. 1 (Monograph 1), 1959.

and to anguish and anxiety. The external conflict is thus accompanied by internal conflict, and if resolution is difficult there may be ego diffusion and identity crisis. Working through the crisis may be a painful and protracted process, often extending into the college years before it is resolved.

Although Erikson does not state that an identity crisis is the normal or expected mode of development, the generalized concept has become so popular that some think an identity crisis is characteristic of adolescence and early adulthood. Erikson's own writing may have inadvertantly contributed to that end, because most of his data come from the consulting room, and as a clinician he spends more time and illustration with conflict and disturbance in development than with a description of normalcy.

But there are other sources. Throughout the centuries many writers have described adolescence as a difficult period. One ancient recorder of the Egyptian scene reported: "Our earth is degenerate . . . .children no longer obey their parents."[11] Aristotle said of adolescents that "their wishes are keen without being permanent, like a sick man's fits of hunger and thirst. They are passionate, irascible, and apt to be carried away by their impulses."[12] More recent description of crisis in adolescence can be found in novels from our Western culture. Among the more memorable ones are Thomas Wolfe's *Look Homeward, Angel,* James Joyce's *Portrait of the Artist as a Young Man,* J. D. Salinger's *Catcher in the Rye,* and John Knowles's *A Separate Peace.* For a long time, sensitive and insightful authors have described the anguish of their own adolescence or that of fictional characters.

Of more recent vintage is the emphasis on a difference between the younger and adult generations, a difference that has been the keynote of both social commentary and declamations by the young. The "generation gap" was one of the bywords of the sixties. Although discussion of the generation gap has not focused specifically on crisis and turmoil, it has reinforced the idea that in

11. Cited by Adelaide M. Johnson, "Juvenile Delinquency," in Silvano Arieti (ed.), *American Handbook of Psychiatry* (New York: Basic Books, 1959), I, 840.

12. *Rhetoric of Aristotle,* trans. J. E. C. Welldon (New York, 1866), pp. 164–166, quoted in Norman Kiell, *The Universal Experience of Adolescence* (New York: International Universities Press, 1964), pp. 18–19.

adolescence we can expect lack of communication, anger, and painful breaking of ties with the past. Thus, there is indirect support of the crisis model.

These ideas have a more powerful impact on most of us because of the growing social problems an industrialized society faces and because of the ensuing social change currently underway. Adults recall with some nostalgia a more peaceful time for growing up, and the remark is often heard, "It's tough to be a teen-ager today." The feeling that the young are especially vulnerable to turmoil may also contribute to the idea that crisis is the most characteristic way of describing the adolescent years.

Within the crisis model are at least four variations of the process that can occur, two of them involving a new integration that represents growth or development and leads to adaptation. The first, and most dramatic, is upheaval and fragmentation followed rather quickly by reorganization on a new level. Some kind of conversion experience would be an example—converting in a conventional Christian way, or turning to Zen Buddhism, or being radicalized in a social and political sense. There are occasions when adolescents get into trouble with the law or school that result in confrontation and perhaps in punishment. These occasions sometimes lead to a reappraisal by the person of his actions, attitudes, values, and goals. These events, unpleasant as they may be in many instances, can be followed by greater maturity and may be regarded some years later as beneficial by the person who was confronted. In a less dramatic way, events in college can serve much the same purpose when they bring the student face to face with new and unsettling reality. Many students at Harvard have been members of the academically elite in secondary school, accustomed to high grades and praise from teachers. For some, a low grade on a theme in expository writing or a failure on the first hour exam can be momentarily shattering. With recovery comes a more realistic self-appraisal and a consideration of new kinds of things the student must do in order to get good grades once again. Sometimes this confrontation forces a change in interests and field of concentration, with new ideas about a future career.

In the second variation, disruption is again followed by reorganization on a new level, but it is attained only slowly and painstakingly; the person moves ahead in some areas, then seems to lose ground again for awhile. Change may be slow to appear and some years may go by before the reorganization is complete. The popularized version of the identity crisis and the sophomore slump are examples. In both cases the person may have a sense of aimlessness, of depression, and of disorganization. He may drop out of school, may lose interest in regular social activities, or may take up new fads of dress and behavior. Some find a reintegration spontaneously, perhaps in a few months, others only with the help of psychotherapy. In some cases the reintegration may take a few years, but for most a new self eventually emerges.

Disruption and upheaval do not always result in reintegration at a new level, and in a third variation there is a return to the same kind or level of personality organization that existed before the crisis occurred. Some individuals, particularly those with certain kinds of neurotic conflicts, go from one crisis to another, following the same pattern each time and not learning from experience. Any developmental change that occurs is minimal. In common parlance, these people are often referred to as perpetual adolescents.

Finally, there is the situation where crisis is followed by increased disorganization and diffusion, then by regression and deterioration. In these cases the psychopathology is usually severe and the outcome can be an attempted or successful suicide or a psychotic withdrawal. For some adolescents and young adults, the academic and social pressures of college awaken old issues that were never settled, and academic failure or a rejection by a friend may precipitate a crisis. A few of our subjects had this difficulty.

There are a number of limitations that apply to the crisis model of development and the material that supports it. The first refers to material in the clinical and psychiatric literature. By and large, the data on which the conclusions are based are from clinical experience, that is, from the consulting room. The bias in the data is the assumption that an accurate picture of healthy or normal functioning can be obtained from a study of disturbed functioning. Implicit is the corollary that health is the absence of symptoms and that to understand the normal we do not need any new conceptions of functioning that is absent in illness situations. This is not to imply that writers like Anna Freud or Erikson are in error, but rather to suggest that it is all too easy to talk as if their conclusions represented the total experience of growth and development.

How much is the adolescent crisis, as portrayed in fiction or biog-

raphy, real or apparent? Few people have described adolescence as
a beautiful period. Most of the writers are sensitive and introspective individuals, who portray the crisis and pain in their characters
in such a way that others can empathize with the feelings. That descriptive ability often comes with people who themselves have been
vulnerable to the vicissitudes of development and have experienced
considerable upheaval in their own adolescent and young adult
days. They are not necessarily characteristic of the general population, however, and their characters may not be typical of adolescence. To be sure, art is a representation of life, but life also
can reflect art in the ideas that people hold about adolescence.

What about the effect of events of the present day, that is, the
generation gap? Quite possibly the idea of a gap has been overdone—
not that differences between the generations do not exist, but that
they have been exaggerated. Joseph Adelson[13] marshals a convinc-
ing argument that a majority of the younger generation do not feel
a great gap and have not significantly altered either their values or
their behavior from those of their parents. The minority who do
feel a gap have been vocal, and their comments have been reinforced
by the unease of liberals in the older generation about the general
state of the world. Consequently, the quiet, non-crisis development
of the majority may be overlooked.

We must also bear in mind that crisis and upheaval can interfere
with development rather than advancing it, either slowing it down
or crippling it in some way. Crisis may prevent a person from utilizing features of the environment that could contribute toward growth.
In the college situation, a student in a severe sophomore slump may
avoid extracurricular activities that would bring interpersonal satisfactions and enhance his skills in dealing with people. He may not
have the inclination to look for new and exciting courses in areas
he is not familiar with and thus may cut off the development of
new interests and possible career opportunities. The student who
spends a good deal of emotional energy trying to achieve a reintegration in his personality may be so impaired that he cannot take
advantage of opportunities that may not occur again. The consequences can be permanent.

Another point comes from our own data. The majority of our

13. Joseph Adelson, "What Generation Gap?" *New York Times Magazine,*
January 18, 1970.

subjects gave no evidence of having experienced the disruption and turmoil characteristic of the adolescent crisis. This was true in the retrospective accounts of their pre-college days and of what we observed while they were at Harvard. We do not mean to imply that they did not have failures, that they did not become depressed, that they did not feel tension. At times these events occurred, but the feelings were limited in time and in the extent to which they affected general personality functioning. Most important of all, the students did not "feel" that they had gone through crisis; they described a sense of integration rather than of disruption.

Possibly some students underwent a crisis they were not aware of or could not recall. Some may have gone through one before Harvard and have become sufficiently integrated that they no longer felt it when we saw them and thus felt no need to report it. On the other hand, our test instruments were varied and our interviews extensive. In all these assessment procedures there should have been enough sensitivity to pick up crisis had it occurred.

The crisis model emphasizes the disruptive effect of too great a disparity between past and present, giving too little attention to those ties with the past which are positive in nature. Although all persons probably have some sense of disparity, the majority have developed relationships with people that were, and still are, satisfying, have taken from these people qualities that they admired, and still reflect those qualities, and have learned skills and techniques for adaptation that they still use. For them, relevant past material is functional in the process of coping with environmental and internal problems. Our data impressed us with the ties our subjects had to the past, although they sometimes altered it, sometimes used it without change. This model of growth, which we call continuity, emphasized a working through of the past, slowly and usually without much drama.

The *continuity model* stresses that significant growth occurs more frequently through finding new applications for successful behavior patterns from the past, through increasing the repertoire of responses, and through modifying or reworking patterns from the past to meet new situations. Though there is change, there is also a sense of sequence or extension. Growth is most likely to occur through a series of small changes and thus to be unobtrusive in nature.

All individuals have many automatic response patterns that occur in the presence of certain stimuli with little or no conscious thought. Generally speaking, these are patterns that have worked in the past and are likely to work again. They come out of the experience of successful adaptation. They are not automatic in the same way as compulsive mechanisms; the latter are defenses against anxiety, the former, ways of coping. Nor are the automatic responses the same as conditioned reflexes, because many of them involved conscious thought and planning in the beginning and the person can usually perceive why and how he uses them. They are automatic in that they occur with minimal cues and do not produce negative feedback.

Growth occurs when the person learns how to transfer effective automatic patterns from the past to new situations. This is *growth by extension*, where common features of situations are recognized, even though in some respects the situations may appear to be quite different. Leaving home for college or for a job provides an opportunity for growth by extension, especially if the person goes some distance socially as well as physically.

Growth occurs when responses that arise out of successful and satisfying experiences in the past are changed to fit the particular characteristics of new situations. This is *growth by modification*. In one form, there is a sharpening or focusing process, as when a person gets deeply into a subject and finds new ideas and new interests. An interest in nature during childhood that has led to a general enjoyment of science in secondary school may lead to concentration in biology and growing interest in animal ecology. From this can come career plans for graduate work in ecology and the development of a life style that involves teaching and research. Continuity with the past is there because science as a field has absorbed the student since childhood. Modification is there because the interest has narrowed to specific aspects of science, although with that narrowing comes also a richer repertoire of responses.

In another form, an alteration takes place, as when a person reworks the values with which he has been reared and establishes new guidelines for his conduct. For example, one of the current preoccupations among younger people is with aggression, with how it should be expressed and controlled. There is a good deal of concern about violence, in war or civil disobedience. There is also concern about the range of situations where passive or nonaggressive behavior is acceptable. In order to develop a consistent set of values, many students are rethinking rather extensively the traditional values that heretofore they had accepted.

Growth also occurs in the development of new patterns of behavior related only indirectly to material from the past, but in the indirectness there is continuity. This is *growth by accretion and exploration.* Again, the area of interests can provide an illustration. One of our students had an opportunity to take courses in the history of art and to join an informal class in watercolors as part of his House activity. He forgot that his mother's father had pursued art as an avocation; however, some part of this was represented, so that unconsciously his choice was related to the past. The material in the courses was new and led to fresh insights about man's creative urges and to the development of talents within the student that may only have been hinted at before. The association with his grandfather's interests was a small bit of continuity that allowed him to expand his interests in a number of areas.

The continuity syndrome, though not so named, was illustrated in a study previously reported in the literature by Roy Grinker. In the late 1950's, he conducted an in-depth study of a sample of students at George Williams College, and his reaction to the experience is worth reporting: "The impact of these interviews on me was startling! Here was a type of young man I had not met before in my role as a psychiatrist and rarely in my personal life. On the surface they were free from psychotic, neurotic, or disabling personality traits. It seemed that I had encountered some mentally 'healthy' men who presented a unique opportunity for study."[14] There was a close relationship between students and their parents. They both partook of the same culture, which emphasized early work, sound religious training, and ideals associated with doing good. Parental values could be accepted without rebellion because of the sincere manifestations of love and consistency toward the child. Identifications were thus favored. Although many of the students would surpass their fathers in terms of education, they

14. Roy R. Grinker, " 'Mentally Healthy' Young Males (Homoclites)," *Archives of General Psychiatry*, 6 (June 1962), 405.

did not thus differentiate themselves from parental values and goals. Almost none of the subjects had acted out rebelliously. Although they felt some conflict with parents during adolescence, there was little to indicate that they felt a disturbing identity crisis. They were able to grow and change without difficulties that precipitated overt conflict. "During easy stages of progression from home, church, YMCA, high school and college, the value systems of their environment remained constant."[15] Grinker felt that one of the key variables in the continuity was the strong set of identifications that the subjects made in early childhood. Not only did ego ideal and superego relate to early identification; so did interests, expressed satisfactions, pressures for achievement, and fears of failure. Faithfulness to the past was striking.

This is an appropriate place to interrupt what is essentially a theoretical discussion and to present the history of one of our students. Ideas about personality development can become sterile unless they are enlivened with the behavior of a real person. Furthermore, the reader should have an opportunity to develop some of his own ideas from case material, against which he can better judge the utility of the concepts presented here.

15. Ibid., pp. 448–449.

Chapter 3 / Jason Jellinec

The subject of our first case study, Jason Jellinec, traveled a great distance, both physically and culturally, when he came to Harvard. He had grown up in a small city of some 25,000 people in the Northern Plains, and the open country of that area was in some contrast to the city atmosphere of Harvard Square. He was reared in farming country with still a touch of the frontier about it. Not many went to college, no one from his family had done so, and there had been little in his early life to prepare him for the cultural sophistication of the urban East. He did not realize it at first, perhaps not even until his junior year and then only vaguely, but he would never be able to go home again. He would visit, to be sure, and enjoy his visits, would spend a summer or two there, but he would never go back there to live.

Many of the people in Jason's hometown traced their roots directly to Eastern and Central Europe. Jason's grandfather had been a fairly high-ranking civil servant in the old country, but his father was lured by opportunities in the new world and came to the United States to be a farmer. His mother followed in two years. They worked hard and reared a large family, with Jason appearing toward the end of the birth order. By the time he arrived, his father's industriousness had enabled him to add a hardware store to his farm holdings and the family had moved into town, but Jason could remember with great pleasure his summers on the farm.

The most important activity of Jason's boyhood was baseball.

He had shown early evidence of good coordination and as soon as he was old enough he joined the Little League. Even before that, one of his earliest memories was of being carried home on his brothers' shoulders after winning a game for his team. His father, thinking such things were foolish, gave him no support in this interest, but his mother in her quiet way encouraged him.

Because his father was aloof and even malicious and ill-tempered at times, Jason was fortunate to have an extended family of brothers and sisters. Most of them lived in the same city; some were married, some were still at home. He took part in their activities and they schooled him in the ways of the world, which his father was unable to do. He talked a good deal about this in the family interview and, as we got to know him, the support of the large family emerged as one of the crucial factors in his development.

Just on the verge of Jason's teens, tragedy struck. His father died quite suddenly, followed only a year later by his mother. The first was a bewildering experience, the second a numbing one. His mother, though firm in discipline and unswerving in her sense of morality, had been a warm and accepting person, with ample resources for her large family. Jason grieved deeply over this event, but the family drew together and helped him slowly weather the pain. There was room for him with a married brother, plus a good deal of solid support and love.

Thus his teen years were not lonely ones, for, in addition to the family interaction, he had a job on weekends, and of course there was the engrossing activity of sports. Jason had not only a lot of natural ability but also a strong desire to win and an enthusiasm that sparked the team spirit. Many thought he might have prospects someday as a big-leaguer, but that idea never was tested. When he was a junior in high school, a businessman in the city, for whom Jason had worked and with whom he had become friendly, talked to him about going to college and particularly to Harvard. This was surprising, because Jason had never been outstanding in school, but the businessman, a person named McCrea, had talked with his principal and teachers, who thought Jason had academic potential even if he had not yet proved it. The upshot of all this was financial backing by Mr. McCrea and some members of the Harvard Club in the state for Jason to go to a small private boarding school in the Midwest, with the hope that he might apply later to Harvard. Although

our story comes only from Jason, it was apparent that Mr. McCrea
was recruiting not just an athlete but someone whose drive and personal appeal made a strong impression. In retrospect, Jason reported to us that he had been excited about the new move, although
worried about his academic ability.

The year at Greenwood Academy was not as overwhelming as
he had feared. He starred at sports and was popular with his classmates. The headmaster and his wife took to him and made him welcome at their house, so that once again he had a kind of extended
family for emotional support. But he did struggle with his courses,
particularly with the writing of themes. Perhaps it was from lack of
practice, perhaps from the effects of growing up and hearing a
foreign language often at home, but Jason received some F's, his
first experience with failure. He went for help, and the English
teacher responded by giving him a weekly session in which the two
of them went over each theme with care. By the end of the year he
was doing acceptable, if not superior, work.

His College Board scores were among the lowest at Greenwood,
but the headmaster felt the scores underrepresented his true ability
and made a strong case for Jason when the admissions man from
Harvard came to the school. Apparently Harvard agreed, and accepted him.

The First Year

Registration took place late in September, but Jason was on hand
earlier for "dorm crew," a paying job provided by the College that
helped him put money away for the coming expenses of the academic year. Money, however, was not the only gain for him. He had a
chance to get advance information about courses, meet some of the
coaches, and start making friends. He was adept at making good contacts and when classes began he felt he knew his way around.

His biggest challenge was in course work and his fall term schedule
was not reassuring. Like most freshmen, he was required to take Expository Writing, known simply as Gen. Ed. In addition, he had a
course in Greek drama, a course in geology because he was interested in the oil situation in his home area, and beginning Slavic, which
he took on the naive assumption that his childhood experience with
a similar language would make the course easy for him.

The writing of papers in Gen. Ed. did not go well. Assignments were vague, like "write an 800-word paper on happiness and things of this sort," as Jason put it. Even though he worked hard, he got poor marks and most of his early papers came back with sharply critical comments on them. But the other courses were also difficult, and Jason reacted to the situation by using two adaptive techniques that were characteristic of him. He sought out his teachers for special help, having quickly realized that they would not come to him, and he scheduled himself for study time in places where he was unlikely to be disturbed. In the former, he was both open and serious, and in the latter he was able to exercise good self-discipline. As a result, he managed to get through the fall term, at least until mid-year examinations. He had never taken three-hour exams before, and many of the questions called for long essay answers. He failed the Slavic exam and got no higher than a C on any of the others.

The Slavic had been a mistake for him, one instance where depending too much on the familiar and the past hindered rather than helped. His difficulty with the other courses could be pinpointed when he recounted the experience of going over one of the exam papers with his section man: "I just didn't have any unity. I didn't follow from one item to another in a logical manner. I jumped all over. And the questions were so broad in that course." Even the year at Greenwood had not prepared him for this cognitive task of organizing a large number of facts in some coherent form that represented a reasonable argument.

Nonetheless, Jason survived academically. His record was not poor enough to bring probation or suspension, and in the spring term he managed without any failures. He was learning slowly how to write a paper or exam question at Harvard. His main adaptive mechanism was still a constructive utilization of the adults in the community, which might be illustrated by his work on a paper for a social science course he had added for the spring term. He was interested in the educational experiences of children in economically disadvantaged sections of Boston and proposed to gather some data from them by interview. He knew little about ways of analyzing his data and found only limited help from books in Lamont Library, so he went to the instructor's office and asked for help.

I just told him that I was wrting this paper and that I had a
lot of information. I didn't take my interviews down on tape
because I didn't have a tape recorder, and also, I never thought
of it at the time. I asked him whether this would work against
me and he said definitely not. He said if you'd taken it down on
tape it might have caused you more trouble because you'd have
so much information you wouldn't know where to start. And
he said this would be a more interesting paper because you're
expressing what you witnessed yourself.

The two talked for an hour, about the paper, the course, and about
Jason's background. He was fortunate in finding an instructor who
was firmly interested in undergraduates, but at the same time Jason
had an earnest manner that usually brought a favorable response
from others.

A variation on this theme took place with the section man in his
geology course who volunteered to sit down with Jason after each
lecture and go over his notes and discuss anything that was not
clear. In the spring interview in which he discussed this incident, he
said he had been quite moved by the giving of time and interest. He
felt that he now had an obligation to return the favor, not to the
section man, but to someone else who might need his help.

Finally, he got on well with the proctor in his dorm, a man who
knew the bureaucratic workings of Harvard to perfection and who
was comfortable and easy with students. The relationship here was
much the same as Jason had had with his older brothers after his
parents' death, but he put something into it as well as receiving
something.

One of the biggest stresses of the freshman year was the decision
to forego baseball. From the beginning, he had worried about his
eligibility and realized how much more time he needed to spend on
studying than did many of his friends in order to get passing grades.
He knew from past experience that baseball would cut deeply into
his time and make it difficult for him to maintain his study schedule. The crucial factor in the decision seemed to be his growing awareness of the value of a college degree. "The only thing that I've got in
mind is that I'm never going to fail out of here, and I know I won't.
I'll put everything else aside if I have to—and just work on my
schoolwork." He found that his scholarship aid would not be in jeop-

ardy if he did not play, which was a relief to him, and he convinced
the coach of the correctness of his decision. All this is not to say
that he did not have regrets, and in the spring interview there was
some nostalgia about his high school days, when sports had been
the center of his life.

Three other aspects of Jason's freshman year must be mentioned.
One was the way in which his world opened up in literature and the
arts. Assignments in his humanities course included some of the
Greek tragedies, and he also had read *Paradise Lost,* which, much to
his surprise, he realized he could understand and appreciate. Also,
he discovered the world of classical music, learning a lot from one
of the students in his entry in the dormitory and going to some concerts of the Boston Symphony Orchestra. The impression he left in
the interview was of sampling, as though he felt he should like this
kind of music but did not yet have an emotional commitment to it.
The important thing, however, was his openness to new experience.

A second theme concerned an interest in and a tentative reaching
out for a better understanding of the ethnic group in which he had
his ancestral roots. He had met another Harvard student who came
from the same background and who introduced him to some people
in Boston who were active in an ethnic society. He went to their
meetings, heard the language again and ate the food, and later told
the interviewer that there was an aspect of his life here that he
wanted in some way to pursue.

The other theme concerns his peer relationships, both with his
fellow students and with a girl back home. We have noted that he
made friends easily and that his adjustment to Harvard was aided
by that fact. He got to know many students, was accepted quite
fully in a number of different social groups, and seemed generally
to be well liked. But Jason did not accept all his fellow students un-
critically. Some he felt went too far in kidding the proctor. Others
were in the "party crowd," drank quite heavily, and were often
loud and boisterous. He wondered in the interviews what some of
these students were trying to prove and indicated that he did not
think he would have much in common with them. Also, behind
his apparent ease with others was some hint of shyness and feeling
of social distance. The only place he had made friends with upper-
classmen was on the athletic field, and he said that he had not taken
the initiative there as much as he should have. He also felt a gulf

between himself and his roommates in terms of grades and academic ability. He wondered about his lack of social skills and whether he really belonged with these people. Few of his friends apparently saw this side of him, and it was mentioned to the interviewer only in passing.

The other aspect of Jason's peer relationships concerned a girl with whom he said he was very much in love. During the summer before his freshman year the romance had become serious, and they contemplated marriage. Nancy planned to become a nursery school teacher and was enrolled in a teachers' college back home. They corresponded frequently all fall and found their feelings for each other to be as strong as ever during Christmas vacation. But they were also more and more aware of the strain induced by being separated and talked of having Nancy transfer to a school in the Boston area, though nothing came of it. By late in the spring both of them were dating other people. Jason said that he did not know which of them was changing, but he did admit that they were growing apart and that they might have made a wrong move in being so serious about each other. He did not break with her during the year, however, and he went home for the summer to straighten out "this little love affair."

Those who know Harvard well may feel at this point that Jason was almost too good to be true and that the interest that faculty and administration took in him seems unreal. Perhaps his was a somewhat unusual experience, but his manner brought helpful responses from others without the arousal of pity, or unease about dependence, or any feeling that giving him extra help was unusual. One might say that he inspired rescue fantasies.

As he prepared to leave for the summer, he felt that he had not changed perceptibly and that he did not want to let Harvard go to his head. He was convinced, however, that Harvard had been "great" for him and would be "even greater" in the future. He felt quite certain that he could "make it" from an academic point of view and that he could play baseball next year.

Personality Functioning

It may be helpful at this point to pause in the case material and note some of the characteristics of Jason's personality that seemed important to us in assessing his development and initial reaction to Harvard. In so doing, some data from various psychological tests can be added and a general personality baseline established for an evaluation of change by senior year.

Jason made friends easily, related well to adults, and was regarded by his peers as a leader, although in his freshman year there was little opportunity for leadership. He also had a certain reserve and shyness at times that kept him from a close emotional involvement with people unless he knew them well. Also, he expressed a strong sense of responsibility toward his fellow man, but as yet had found little opportunity to put it into practice.

We might infer that his capacity to relate to people came from the relationship with his mother, who was a warm, supporting person, though firm in setting limits for him. In the interviews he showed little conscious identification with his father, yet, interestingly enough, he did not dwell on his father's coldness and dominance. It is possible, though we had no direct evidence for this, that on an unconscious level he had a positive identification with his father's success and ability to achieve in a new land. In his older brothers he found much that was missing in his father and turned to them with many of his problems, as well as receiving support and affection from them.

He may also have been aided in his development by a full grief reaction at the time his parents died, because he had been able to bring out his guilt, especially in regard to his mother, and work it through. When he came to college, he could approach adults without projecting bitterness into the relationship or making demands that might have been based on unresolved guilt or anger and attempts at restitution.

For another characteristic, Jason had a strong but realistic sense of self-esteem. Although he had won many honors on the athletic field and knew he would win more, he also realized that many other students had better intellectual capacities and were more sophisticated in the ways of the world than he. On his freshman "Who Am I?" test, he described himself as reasonable, affectionate, trustworthy, likeable, conscientious, and shy. He also said that he was "a person who at times gets too moody," who finds it difficult to concentrate, and whose mind "changes too much." Although these last phrases indicate some self-doubt, it was subdued and did not blunt his view of himself as an effective person. In the Rorschach interpretation, McArthur noted that he had "a great deal of thrust" and was at the emotional stage when the expression of strong inner resources in physical activity was both appropriate and useful and aided his positive feelings about himself.

Jason had a rather well-integrated set of values, interests, and goals. He talked about a possible career in education as a teacher in secondary school. He wanted a wife and family and even in his freshman year was looking forward to the day when he would have children to raise. On the Strong Vocational Interest Blank his highest scores were on Group VI of the scales, often characterized as the social service group. In contrast, his scores were generally low on scales for the professions and the natural sciences.

He stressed industriousness, thrift, conscientiousness, and integrity, and had a set of essentially conservative moral principles. This was reflected in his score on the religious scale of the Allport-Vernon-Lindzey Scale of Values, which was higher than those of most of his classmates. He described several incidents in his childhood when he had been punished for lying or stealing, minor offenses to some extent but treated seriously by his mother as a breach of values. He had been punished for these, but the incidents had not later been held over his head. Also, he viewed his mother as having lived what she preached and could accept much of the same value system for himself. We were struck by the fact that interests, goals, and values fitted together in his personality in an adaptive rather than a restrictive way.

There were a number of effective coping mechanisms. When Jason had setbacks from the environment, his reactions were more likely to be counteractive than depressive, and in general he was more on the optimistic than the gloomy side of things. There was a hint of depressive tendencies in the "Who Am I?" test, but it seemed to be in a minor key.

In handling impulses, he had an outlet for aggression in athletic competition that was sufficient and satisfying. He was not a prude about sexual behavior, but he set limits on it; that is, he would have intercourse only within the context of a close relationship.

He was adept at polling the environment, at finding out what was expected and how other people were likely to react. He was attuned to people's opinions and had an uncanny capacity to find those people in the environment who were most representative of what was going on. He was also oriented to present time and place and to the tasks at hand. He could put his tasks into a hierarchy and devote his energies to those highest on the list. As he said, he would put everything else aside in order not to flunk out of Harvard.

Finally, he was able to share his feelings with others, not with an air of self pity but with an air of openness about painful affect that brought supporting responses from other people. He was able to share feelings with both peers and adults, and he was also able to listen to both, enabling them to talk about their own fears and tensions, so that the experience was indeed a sharing one. Again, the sources for this coping mechanism seemed to lie within his large and close-knit family, where feelings were expressed easily and age made little distinction for understanding another.

We might close this section with an interesting overall characterization of our subject which comes from the Rorschach interpretation. Dr. McArthur, the examiner, reported: "The Rorschach style of this man is rather precisely that of the Greek heroes; a little bigger than life, and therefore a little less human . . . . All of his inner resources are concerned with the question of the role of the Greek hero. In particular, he likes to talk about gods in the Greek sense and their role of superiority and watching over, but at the same time being welcomed and being guarded and protected by their people."

Although Jason may have been influenced in his imagery by his course in Greek drama and may thus have used material available in his environment, we cannot help but be impressed that he chose this imagery in contrast to many other references he had available. The theme of the Homeric Hero is a symbolic way of saying that he had certain ways of regarding himself that aided his adaptation. We have no evidence that the theme was explicit in his consciousness, but it acted on him in subtle and impelling ways. It helps to explain his easy commerce with others; he felt strong and competent and not threatened by others. He also had a kind of humility, something more than *noblesse oblige,* that involved a sense of duty and responsibility and concern for others.

The theme helps to explain his self-esteem, his feeling that most battles he would win, as if that were part of his nature. Also, it provides a clue to his realistic self-appraisal, for part of his strength lay in knowing how good he was in most things, no more and no less than in actuality.

The theme also gives us some perspective on his idealism and goal-directed activity. He felt confident that he could accomplish certain ends, not that they would be given easily to him, but that they would be his with effort. Perhaps, in this connection, we have a hint of coming things, of his ability to make the geographical and cultural leap from the Plains to Cambridge.

Jason as an Upperclassman

During the summer Jason was at home, touching base with the family, earning some money on a construction job that Mr. McCrea had arranged for him, and re-establishing his romance with Nancy.

The job provided something more than money because it cast Jason in the role of college student among generally uneducated workers. They asked his opinion on all kinds of issues and were envious rather than antagonistic toward his status. He felt, as a consequence, that he had all the more to prove himself in the rough-and-tumble aspects of the work-gang culture. He got into a fairly serious wrestling match, almost a fight, one day, and his reactions reflected the theme we mentioned just above.

> I was just determined not to get beaten. I don't know why I felt that way—perhaps a little bit of fear, perhaps the fear of not being looked up to in a certain respect, since I had been losing this sort of prestige I had in talking to them about what school was like. I was determined to beat him—it was in the back of my mind all the while I was fighting that I just had to beat him or else that would be it. I think this is something that is in my mind all the time, no matter whether I'm playing sports or what I'm doing. I like to win.

Although the romance with Nancy deepened, Jason still had some doubts about it at the end of the summer, about whether it would really last until they could be married. When he returned to school, however, he was desperately lonely for her, a feeling that lasted some weeks.

Sophomore year was a settling year, marked by a slow but noticeable improvement in his grades and his ability to write; he found he could do much better on long papers than on short ones. Also, social relations began to attract him as a field of concentration, as he took the introductory course and one on social deviance. He had a growing awareness that he could earn acceptable grades, and his fears of flunking out receded. At the time, these changes were small ones, but in the long run they were of great importance because he was developing intellectual competence to go along with his interpersonal and athletic competence.

One of the more important events of that year took place outside the academic realm. It began through a conversation with some students from Phillips Brooks House, who described a tutoring program for youngsters from economically deprived and educationally poor areas of Boston and asked Jason to participate. His response was enthusiastic, which is not surprising from what we know of his idealism and desire to help others. But his action also illustrated one of his weaknesses, the tendency to say yes to things quite quickly, to start activities with enthusiasm and then sometimes find that he had taken on more than he could handle. It is one example of where his control mechanisms were ineffective. On this venture, however, he carried through.

He enjoyed working with younger boys and found real challenges in his tutoring task, not the least of which was in developing a motivation for school work. Thus, he saw his role as being a counselor as much as being a teacher. No matter what he did, some of the boys made no progress. But they liked him, and a few showed substantial increases in their school grades. The tutoring took time and was voluntary, but at the end of the year Jason commented that it had been one of the best experiences of the year. He knew he had made mistakes, which he could correct, and he had learned about having limited goals. As we thought about his experience and his reactions to it, the benefit seemed to derive from the way in which his idealism had been tempered with reality, an experience that was new for him and would have important implications in experiences in his senior year.

As the year progressed, Jason planned on going out for the baseball team, feeling assured that he could combine that with an acceptable academic record. When spring tryouts arrived, he found that he had lost none of his skill, and he made the team without any question. In fact, his presence helped turn a good team into one of the best that Harvard had fielded in years. That was due in no small measure to the fact that he put all he had into the game and imparted his enthusiasm to his teammates.

He was tested that spring in another way. Some of the sports writers singled him out for comment when he made an occasional misplay; his fame had preceeded him, and they said they expected better. Jason was annoyed, because he felt he was doing well and that the criticism reflected on the team as well as on him. He worried that other team members as a result might resent him, but the fact that he was basically a team man saved him, and his fellow players rallied to his support rather than rejecting him. Again, however, it was a tempering experience; he was forced to realize the responsibilities that go with fame. He had not been as vulnerable to this before.

One other incident of the sophomore year should be mentioned. In spite of his social background, he was sought after by the two fraternities and some of the Final Clubs. He was flattered, yet felt uncomfortable because he did not like the exclusiveness of the clubs or what he considered to be time-wasting activities. He eventually joined one of the fraternities, but it never became a significant part of his Harvard life. The incident is important because it indicates his basic ability to bridge the cultural gap between his rural background and the Eastern Establishment. That he did not get carried away with it says something about his subtle reserve in relations with others, which still persisted.

Events of the ensuing summer provided the opening rounds of Jason's most painful period at Harvard and of some significant strides in self-insight. When he went home he found a cool reception from Nancy, which baffled and then infuriated him. She no longer wanted to be his little girl or to have him try to mold her, she said. He went off by himself and "bawled like a baby," then got mad at her, then tried to get at her by dating other girls—all to no avail, for she rejected him. So he left and came back east to look for a job. The experience shook him. It hurt because he had always felt she was one person who could understand and accept him, as a serious type, yet one who could have fun. Other girls thought he was too serious. He also wondered about his skill in handling relationships with women. His pride and his self-esteem were hurt more than ever before.

He found a job in a small hotel on Cape Cod that was frequented in the summer by members of the ethnic society he had become acquainted with in his freshman year. He liked them and thought that in the course of the summer he could learn more about his cultural heritage. Also, the job paid well. At any rate, for a time he forced Nancy from his mind and reimmersed himself in childhood memories of language and custom.

But Nancy's loss had turned him more toward introspection and to thinking about self-control; from this came conflict about handling sexual impulses. He had had sexual relations with Nancy but still thought of himself as "pure," and now he was worried that he would become corrupt. He wanted a girl to replace the emotional aspects of the relationship with Nancy, yet he also felt strong physical desires he was reluctant to gratify in the free and easy ways available around Boston. The more he looked inward the more depressed he became and the more aimlessness he felt.

> I'm getting a feeling of disappointment at myself because I haven't been working as hard as I used to. I've been very frustrated and annoying to my roommates. I've been giving them sort of a hard time because I feel that they're spending so damn much time studying, and doing a good job, and getting good grades on hour exams, and here I'm really not. I'm just running here and there and not settling down as they can. This concern about not working as effectively as I should be, academically, has been bothering me. I can't sit down and write a paper with pleasure. I have to sit down and skim over some reading which I haven't done to pick out some points.

The process of self-understanding, as well as the resolution of some of his problems, was aided by one of his courses, called the Analysis of Interpersonal Behavior, or Soc. Rel. 120, as everybody knew it, where group discussion was the teaching technique. At first he felt inhibited in the discussion, but as the year progressed he began to face issues in himself that previously had been pushed aside and to talk about them. The course certainly helped to loosen him up, but it also gave him confidence.

The key integrative experience of the year, however, came in a tutorial experience where he did some independent study. The tutor was a sympathetic, understanding man, as well as a real scholar, who was comfortable in talking about either Jason's personal problems or his intellectual concerns and whose advice was indirect but helpful. Jason found in this man what he had found in a number of others in the past, someone who had nurturant qualities but who also encouraged Jason's autonomy. When he looked back over the year from the vantage point of late spring, he felt that in no small measure his growth during the year rested on the discussions he had with his tutor.

Finally, in the spring he met a girl from a neighboring college on a blind date and found once again a woman who understood him. It was of some interest to the interviewer that references to Nancy steadily declined from this point. Jason was cautious about the new relationship with Betty, not wishing to be hurt again, and his ambitions were sufficiently compelling to make him wary of entanglements. But they dated steadily during the spring, and by the time the term ended he was speaking very warmly of her.

All these things had made Jason think not only of what he was like as a person and of the matter of impulse control, but also of the way he related to people in general. Other than with Nancy, he could not recall any relationships that had been deep. He also thought of his difficulty in saying no.

I always felt as though I owed somebody something. If somebody ever did something for me I felt as though I had to do something in return. Whether friends present mother images or what I don't know, but the feeling does exist, and yet I think I understand it more now. I find that in not catering to people, in not being so willing to do things for them, and to repay them, I find that they appreciate me more. I can see it within them, on their faces and in their actions. And I find that I'm more relaxed, they're more relaxed. I get myself involved in a lot of things because I find it hard to say no. As a result I find myself getting mad and depressed and moody because I'm not

in control of the situation. But I think I'm starting to get
things under control and getting a little more direction.

Two final points concern athletics and academics. Jason talked
relatively little in his junior interviews about athletics and baseball, even though his success there continued undiminished and
the interviewer gave him ample opportunity to bring up the topic.
Other things took first place in his attention. He did talk quite a
bit, however, about his course work. He felt that he was no longer
studying just to get through Harvard but for an interest in his subjects. Old doubts still lingered, however: "I still don't feel as competent as I should. I don't know why—whether it links to my high
school experience, or the language situation in my early years, or
growing up with people who never went to college. Yet I feel as
though I've got a good start and it may lead to something."
He did have an A and some B's and even thought of himself as
someone who might write an honors thesis. In this matter his tutor
encouraged him.

It was through his tutor's efforts that he got a job that summer
interviewing people who were to be relocated in an urban renewal
project in Boston. The research project was interested in the impact
of relocation on the social structure of the major ethnic groups involved. Jason's job was to go into the community, gain the trust
of the residents, and explore with them a number of areas in their
lives. His outgoing manner and emotional warmth gave him an advantage in this task, and he often found it difficult to get away from
a family. Often he went back for visits that were not required by the
interviewing schedule, and he felt he knew far more about these
people than his field notes indicated. He also realized that he had
good material for an honors thesis if he could find some way to organize his data and put it in an acceptable conceptual framework.
Really, he had the problem of too much data. On this note of excitement, coupled with anxiety and frustration, he began his senior
year.

The fall term had not gone too far when Jason was ready to call
his tutor and say, "Forget the whole thing." But he was up against
someone who knew that successful intellectual work sometimes involves pain and who would not let him off the hook.

I have so much respect for him that I couldn't do it. He feels that this is a very important thing and I can see why it's very important to write this thesis—even though I have to muster the energy to get going. He has been pounding it into me. He says, "You know I'm one person you can come to and you don't have to put on any front or airs. But just one thing, you've got to write a thesis. One thing I'm going to hold you to and nothing else. This is one thing I've got to play the teacher role on and hold you to." So whenever I start thinking about not writing a thesis I snap out of it quite quickly.

The problem, however, was not just organization; there was something more personal in it. As he got deeply into the lives of the people he interviewed and into the conflict between the generations, he had a resurgence of feelings about his family and childhood and his ethnic background. This brought up again the question of his identity and how he fitted into a world that was different from that in which he had been reared. Struggling with the thesis mirrored a struggle about identity that had been going on during his years at Harvard and now was in the open and ready for resolution.

I was reading some stuff the other night on the conflict between generations, and I got very melancholy about this thing and started thinking about my own family situation, and about Mother. She just happened to fit into this thing, how well she brought up the children, what type of person she was, and how mean Dad was to her. I was really getting a feeling of what these people are like that I interviewed, how close to nature they are, and how warm, and then I thought how warm Mother was. This stuff just brings home so many things that I have experienced and seen in my own family that it's unbelievable. It brought out very personal things which I'm sure have been responsible for my own character. And the only misgiving I have is will I be able to capture these feelings on paper.

Although the personal aspect of the situation presented a problem for Jason, it was also important as a motivating force in finishing his thesis. When it was submitted, Jason had more proof of how far he had come, in this case intellectually.

While Jason struggled with his thesis, his romance with Betty progressed, though at times unevenly. During the summer he had asked her to marry him, but she had responded with a certain reserve. She knew about Nancy and how Jason had been hurt. She too had been badly hurt in a previous love affair and wanted to wait to see if the present relationship was secure. Finally in the fall she said yes, but they agreed it would be best to wait until the thesis was completed and the baseball season finished. In the meantime, they were learning how to get along together. She was not awed by his athletic prowess and brought to him a kind of emotional reality-testing that he did not always like but that helped him nonetheless. At first, when she criticized him, he felt it meant that she did not think he was any good and reacted by being hurt and angry; the strain of writing the thesis made it worse. But during the winter Jason told the interviewer they could now disagree with each other without losing respect or losing the trust and love they had for each other. But they did have some bad moments during fall and winter.

In the spring they suddenly seemed to have a real breakthrough in their relationship, of a lasting consistency in communication and trust. He could not understand why until the interviewer noted that it had occurred at about the time he turned his thesis in. Betty had typed it for him, so she too had felt tension associated directly with the work. Jason's reaction at this notation of sequence was first to be startled, then to look happy, as though a number of things had suddenly fallen into place. From then on, plans for the wedding seemed to move smoothly.

Relatively little emphasis has been given in these last two years of Jason's career at Harvard to athletic competition, but the writing only reflects the emphasis on events that Jason himself made in the interviews. He continued to enjoy playing baseball and to share the good spirits on the team. He still liked to win and did everything he could to bring that about. Talk about his being good enough for the major leagues persisted, and Jason often considered that move as an alternative to the other, more intellectual career line. In his senior year some pro scouts made tempting offers, but Jason finally eliminated pro ball with only minor misgivings. He knew there was some doubt as to how far he could go, and any-thing less than the major leagues would be unacceptable to him. He also knew that his playing days would be limited and that when they were over he would have a major portion of his life yet to fill. As graduation neared, he decided instead to accept an offer from a firm with extensive overseas commitments and to work for a year. That would provide money and a chance to travel, and at the end of that time he would come back to Harvard Business School, where he had been accepted for graduate work, and hope for a career in personnel management.

Just before graduation the interviewer asked Jason how things had balanced out for him at Harvard, and his thoughts were as follows:

> I've always felt myself to be a person very interested in what goes on around me, very aware of people. Like the rest of my family, being from a rural background, anything we saw was new and different. Our appreciation of things was probably heightened because of this. We're more open to accept things than a lot of people. I feel that my ability to appreciate things and analyze them in more intellectual terms has been sharpened somewhat.

> I can look back and see the advantages in having secured this education. It's been the greatest thing in the world because it's opened so many doors. I would never have been so definite on a vocation; at least I wouldn't have gotten into a good graduate school. I probably would have wandered around with baseball and been very disappointed with myself. Well, the academic has gone ahead of the athletic.

> As far as my attitude goes I don't think it's changed that much, except toward athletics. As far as just working, plodding, making sure that I do an honors job—that hasn't changed.

Extent of Personality Change

Depending on the view one takes, it could be said that Jason chang-ed a great deal or hardly at all. In a social sense, he made great strides from the small-town boy of the Plains to the rather sophisticated

Harvard honors graduate. As noted at the very beginning of his case presentation, he could never go home again to live. He had been accepted by the upper-middle-class New England social group. The girl he was to marry could be so identified, and Jason felt comfortable with her family and they with him. His tutor came from that group, and the two of them had become close friends. Others in the Harvard administration or in Boston liked and respected Jason and felt that he could be part of their world if he wished. His knowledge of literature, the arts, and music, and his general range of intellectual ideas had increased enormously. Although he knew he would never be an academic, he did not feel second-class in intellectual matters. When he left Harvard, he had an ease in manner that suggested he could be at home almost anywhere. Furthermore, there had been little in his background to prepare him for this change or to suggest that it might take place.

In terms of personality structure, Jason changed gradually and to a much smaller degree. He arrived at college with an unusually mature capacity to give and take with others, but some minor changes did occur. The Rorschach indicated that a greater ability to control his reactions to outer stimuli had been achieved, so that he could be appropriately natural about these reactions. The interviews and also the FIRO test indicated that by senior year he was better able to respond to others in the sense of intimacy, as Erikson uses the term. The relationship with Betty showed that he could accept her as an independent person and give of himself to her, with less emphasis on the self-enchancing qualities of such giving. Jason's skill with people thus became fine-tuned rather than amplified.

Jason might be characterized as an effective optimist; his self-esteem was high in his freshman year and remained so throughout. He saw himself as adaptable and secure. At times he expressed self-doubts, and certainly in his junior year he went through a process of self-examination, yet he seemed to limit this introspection and to prevent it from ever reaching the point of self-denigration. There were indications that he occasionally used the defense of denial against certain aspects of his inner nature, but it was not a pronounced defense. In his senior "Who Am I?" test, the hints of depression and tension had given way to statements reflecting a constructive use of his talents in occupational and social life. The change in his self-esteem therefore tended toward a somewhat more accurate assessment of himself rather than any striking increase.

His general appearance was cheerful, and when depressed periods came, they were usually precipitated by environmental events; he handled them by immersing himself in some kind of work or physical activity. Mood swings were not extreme or frequent.

His values, interests, and goals showed relatively little change. The profile on the Strong Vocational Interest Blank was similar to the freshman year, with the high scores on occupations oriented toward social service. He still thought about teaching or guidance work, and if he went into business he planned on a career in personnel administration.

The change that did take place was qualitative, in the conscious mobilization of his energies toward goal attainment, clearly evident in his stories for the Thematic Apperception Test. Although plots of the stories were similar in the freshman and senior years, in the later stories the hero took some direct action to bring about the desired end or goal. The difference lay in the extent to which the mobilization of energy had become autonomous rather than furnished primarily by someone else. Mr. McCrea had made it possible for Jason to go to Greenwood and to Harvard. Jason would make and implement his own plans from now on.

The two most important psychological events in his Harvard career that helped him move toward greater autonomy occurred during his senior year in the work on his thesis. As he re-experienced the grief he felt at his mother's death, he could at the same time internalize the strong qualities in her personality and integrate them as an enduring part of his own. Also, he molded his ethnic background to his present and future needs, because in the people he interviewed he could see strengths that had helped them adjust to the new world.

In his tutor, Jason found a father surrogate whom he could both love and admire. With this man's encouragement and high standards, Jason was able to carry out the most difficult intellectual task of his life. But the man was also a real friend, and Jason identified with his personal as well as his intellectual qualities. The two of them talked a great deal about Jason, who was able to share his inner feelings and at the same time know that the tutor continued to accept him and like him as a person. This helped greatly in the final resolution of his identity concerns.

Jason came to Harvard with coping mechanisms that worked well, and once again the changes were subtle ones. There was some conflict about his sexual impulses in his junior and senior years, and he continued to feel uneasy about sexual expression not associated with a situation of fidelity. But in general he was more comfortable with his impulses.

By senior year, Jason felt a greater intellectual mastery of the world, primarily a broadening by accretion rather than by an alteration in cognitive style. He just knew a lot more; he still used a somewhat literal, rather than abstract, approach to planning. In this respect he was different from many of our subjects, who used abstract thinking as a way of independent scrutiny. Jason still learned through imitation and identification, but the increase in facts enabled him to plan appropriately in a world that had become more complex. He also changed by greater acceptance of the control he experienced over others. He had always controlled others in leadership roles and continued to do so, only now he felt more comfortable in doing so, because he realized that it was often necessary and appropriate.

Finally, some undifferentiated anxiety appeared in the senior year, as evidenced by signs on the Rorschach, on a manifest anxiety scale, and on the unconscious strain scale from the Myers Briggs Type Indicator. We are not quite sure how to account for this. The interviews indicated a number of possible determinants for this increase in anxiety, but none were definitive. It could have come from deeper issues in his personality of which we were not aware. Whatever the source, he managed it well and did not let it interfere with productive effort; his management-of-tension mechanisms were flexible and effective.

In general, he was helped in adapting by his ability to relate to people, but, more specifically, he was adept at polling what was going on and what was expected and in identifying with key people at each stage of his development. He was quick to know when he was doing something wrong and to seek the right people in the environment who might help him correct it. In his early days at Harvard, this device became particularly helpful in the academic sphere. The Harvard environment has many sources of help, but a student must seek them out for himself; if he does, the response from instructors is usually most helpful. Jason knew how to do this. The ability to identify with people, particularly adults, may have gone back to his childhood when his relations with his father were poor and he turned to older brothers, coaches, and others. He must have had some good relationships for later models. As we have noted, he was able to take from people without using them, for he always gave to them in return. He was not instrumental in his object relations. The crucial identification figure of his career, his tutor, who helped him toward personal insight and growth and provided a model for intellectual mastery, also became his friend.

Another strong mechanism lay in his use of activity, particularly physical activity, to reduce tension, express impulses, enchance his self-esteem, and relate to people. Jason is a good example of the manner in which athletics can serve multiple adaptive functions for a person who has the necessary physical attributes. The process of winning brought a sense of competence and enhanced self-esteem, but he also learned the reality factor that "you can't win them all." He knew that the necessity for teamwork and the support of teammates required control of self-interest in the service of team effort. He had the experience of expressing anger under controlled conditions and did not carry a grudge when the game was over. He also found that success is often associated with hard work, physical pain, and fortitude and was able to generalize this lesson to activities other than athletics. Physical activity became a way not only of handling stress but also of providing a continuing adaptive process.

The reader may still feel that Jason Jellinec was almost too good to be true, but we studied many other students who in their own way exhibited a continuity with the past and a steady but gradual pattern of change. He was unusual in his capacity to adapt, and much of what he did at Harvard was exciting, but he was not unique and he was not perfect. He did seem a bit larger than life at times, but so do many people when there is an opportunity to study their lives closely.

Chapter 4 / Variables for Assessing Change

Any single case history is not sufficient in itself to generate all the ideas or variables that a researcher might find useful in understanding personality change during the college years. But the case of Jason Jellinec can serve a number of purposes at this point. It can give the reader the flavor of the data we worked with and indicate the particular approach we used in analyzing case history material. At the same time, the case provides some raw material for speculation about factors that might be important in change or in the process of adaptation. Our discussion of the Jellinec data singled out such factors as interpersonal relations, self-esteem, interests and goals, and coping mechanisms and indicated how these factors were important in understanding Jellinec's behavior. Although the Jellinec case was the first one we analyzed in depth, these same factors appeared in many other students in our group of forty and led us to the conclusion that six major variables were the key ones in our data. These variables will be described in detail, with emphasis on the theoretical description of each variable and illustrative data from the "paper and pencil" tests of our survey sample, from cases in our smaller sample, or from Jason Jellinec.

Object Relations

The importance of Jason Jellinec's skill in relating to people suggests that some variable concerned with interpersonal relations is central to personality change during college. We think the term *object relations,* is sufficiently broad to encompass a variety of behaviors observed in Jellinec and many of our other subjects.

The term comes basically from psychoanalytic theory, although we have modified or restricted its use to human relationships as against nonhuman ones. We also will limit the term to those aspects that are observable patterns of behavior. Object relations thus concern the emotional relationships a person has with other people. The quality of a relationship is important, but so, to a certain extent, are the number of relationships. Good object relations mean the capacity of a person to give and to accept emotional involvement with others, especially in the giving and receiving of love with the same or opposite sex. The term also refers to the ability to form stable identifications with peers, and particularly with adults. Also involved is the capacity to vary responses to others according to the social circumstances, limiting or opening up behavior as the situation demands. Not only are individual relationships included, but also a concern for the social group and the ability to take social responsibility.

One aspect of object relations particularly pertinent to the years of the life cycle covered by college is that of *intimacy.* The term is an important one in Erik Erikson's scheme of life stages, following next after identity formation. Erikson defines it as "the capacity to commit himself to concrete affiliations and partnerships and to develop the ethical strength to abide by such commitments even though they may call for significant sacrifices and compromises."[1] When intimacy develops in relationships between the sexes, it involves a true genitality, in contrast to the previous developmental period where much of sexual life is of the identity-searching kind. The crisis that can occur if there is an interference with intimacy is that of isolation, the opposite of a willingness to share mutual trust.

College provides a favorable opportunity for change and growth in object relations. To be sure, the student has reached an age when he is given increasing amounts of freedom and responsibility, but the very structure of college life gives him occasion to think about and

1. Erik H. Erikson, *Childhood and Society,* 2nd. ed. (New York: W. W. Norton, 1963), p. 263.

to explore new ways of interacting with other people and to rework past object relationships before major social commitments, such as marriage and career, are made. Jellinec agonized over his relationship with Nancy, but because of both psychological and physical distance he could not change the relationship into a truly reciprocal one. When he met Betty, she helped him in the give and take of an intimate relationship that eventually led to marriage.

Although certain other features of college life that affect object relations may appear obvious, they are worth considering for a moment. Most students are given one or more roommates, usually strangers, and have the task of learning how to live with somebody in close quarters, physically and emotionally. The problems in such living are to adjust one's needs, interests, and habits with those of others and to control aggression. Certainly in his freshman year Jason found this difficult at times. A student also has the task of developing affectionate ties and learning how to share things in friendship. For most students, these are not new experiences, especially for those who have attended boarding school or who have been reared with siblings of proximate age, but having a roommate can make the problem of interpersonal adaptation more intense than previously.

Living arrangements at Harvard further accentuate the matter of roommate adjustment. In the Houses, rooming is in suites, each with bedrooms, living room, and toilet. Houses are divided into entries, with two or three suites on each floor of an entry; the contrast, of course, is the traditional long-corridor plan. The entry and suite arrangement inhibits casual mingling and the extension of friendship to other students who live nearby. Not uncommonly, we found that students in a particular suite did not even know the names of other students in the same entry, sometimes even on the same floor.

We cannot tell how much this arrangement affected interpersonal adaptation as compared with other colleges. For whatever reason, the interviews over the four years dwelt a good deal on the vicissitudes and satisfactions of the roommate relationships.

On a formal and informal basis college provides an opportunity for interaction with the opposite sex. Some girls view going to college as an opportunity to find an eligible marriage partner, and the traditional fraternity and sorority system has had the covert goal of bringing together men and women of like social class and background. The dating game is a social phenomenon that grew out of college life. Dating serves a variety of needs for each partner—companionship, prestige-seeking, sexual gratification, as well as selection of spouse[2]—but meeting members of the opposite sex and seeking close relationships with them is a major concern of most young adults.

Finally, extracurricular activities—clubs, politics, theater, newspaper, and particularly sports—provide opportunities for social interaction and also require participants to be able to work together. There are important social rewards in these areas, often hallowed by tradition, and hence the pressure for interpersonal adaptation is increased.

We might note that the form of extracurricular activities may have changed some in recent years. Some coaches report greater difficulty in recruiting people for organized sports, and some of the traditional club activities have less support. At the same time, political activity has increased and so has interest and participation in projects that have immediate social implications, such as Jellinec's tutoring. The particular content or form of extracurricular activities is not crucial to the point we are making. Both a decade ago and now, the college situation has provided a chance to get involved in things other than academic, and such involvement is often interpersonal in nature.

There are also difficulties in the college situation that in one way or another interfere with interpersonal relationships. Heavy academic demands may cause a student to eschew dating or to limit it to only a few occasions a year. Many of our subjects, especially in the freshman year, said that they just did not have time for formal dates. This is undoubtedly too simple a reason. More likely it was pressure of competition, of immediate moment with one's fellow students and in future perspective for graduate school admission. When personal sense of competition is reinforced by explicit or implicit expectations of the college, progress in learning about object relations can be retarded.

It is of some interest in this regard that many of our students, as freshmen, felt uneasy about Radcliffe women, because they saw

2. Rebecca S. Vreeland, "The Development of Heterosexual Relationships in College," in John M. Whitely and Hazel Sprandel (eds.), *The Growth and Development of College Students,* Student Personnel Series no. 12 (Washington, D.C.: American Personnel and Guidance Association, 1970), pp. 31–35.

them as intellectual competitors, and as strong ones at that. Radcliffe women were regarded as less available and less desirable dates than students from neighboring women's colleges. The fear of intellectual dominance by Radcliffe students declined steadily, however, through the four years.

When our study was conducted, the College, through parietal rules, restricted times when students could entertain women in their rooms. But students began to question and object to the imposition of parietal rules; they argued that the College should not extend its influence into the social aspects of a person's life. One motivation behind the ensuing controversy was the belief that parietal rules unduly limit opportunity to make close, natural relationships with the opposite sex. Students said they wanted greater freedom to explore and learn about how to get along with girls.

As a counterpoint to these general and descriptive remarks about object relations, some data from the questionnaire study, using the larger random samples from both classes, are relevant. These data indicate that our students were concerned about relationships with others, with women, and adults as well as male peers.

Prior to matriculation, all subjects were asked about their expectations concerning Harvard—what they hoped to derive from the experience. In the senior year they were asked the same question—what they had derived. Each time they put in their own words the three most important things they expected or later experienced. The answers fell into twelve categories, which in turn could be combined in three major areas: academic, interpersonal, and personal growth. The results in Table 1 show that interpersonal and personal matters assumed greater importance than academic ones over the four years.

Similar results came from the question: "In which of the following areas do you expect to receive (did receive) your greatest satisfactions at Harvard?" (Check one). Eleven categories were presented after the question, which we later grouped into academic, extracurricular, and interpersonal areas. The results, shown in Table 2, are once again in the direction of the interpersonal over the academic.

Finally, students were asked what they thought their major problems would be (were) at Harvard, checking yes or no for each problem listed. The results, shown in Table 3, indicate that academic problems were less important than anticipated, interpersonal ones more so.

Table 1

*First of three most important things to be
derived (were derived) from Harvard experience
(Random Samples, Classes of 1964 and 1965)*

	Freshman Year		Senior Year	
Academic				
Get a liberal education, get culture				
Learn a specific subject, prepare for work or graduate school				
Prestige and reputation				
Become creative				
Get good grades	400	(69%)	116	(34%)
Interpersonal				
Meet different kinds of people				
Learn to understand others				
Have fun or good time	48	(9%)	70	(21%)
Personal growth				
Find myself, identity search				
Find meaning, goals, or outlook for life				
Develop maturity, learn to take responsibility				
Change my personality	129	(22%)	152	(45%)
TOTAL	577		338	

Note: Difference between freshman and senior year is significant by chi square at $< .01$

Self-Esteem

A number of references were made in the previous chapter to the fact that Jason Jellinec had a high and realistic sense of self-esteem, which aided him in his ability to deal effectively with new situations. It was a common finding in our total sample, both of case history subjects and of the survey group. We use the term to mean

Table 2

*Area where student expects to receive (did receive)
greatest satisfaction at Harvard
(Random Samples, Classes of 1964 and 1965)*

	Freshman Year		Senior Year	
Academic				
Formal course work				
Informal study or research				
Individual artistic or literary work	358	(65%)	120	(35%)
Extracurricular				
Life of the dorms and Houses				
Participation in student activities				
Athletics	46	(8%)	70	(21%)
Interpersonal				
Bull sessions				
Parties and social life				
Dating				
Close friendships with other students				
Getting acquainted with a wide				
variety of students	145	(27%)	151	(44%)
TOTAL	549		341	

Note: Difference between freshman and senior year is significant by chi square at < .01

a feeling of satisfaction with oneself, of self-respect, and of worth-whileness. In any person self-esteem varies over time, that is, it fluctuates, and therefore the intensity and the frequency of the fluctuation must be kept in mind in a clinical assessment of personality. People can be differentiated from each other, however, on the general level of self-esteem. What we must consider is the mean

Table 3

Areas expected to be (found to be) major problems at Harvard (Random Samples, Classes of 1964 and 1965)

	Freshman Year		Senior Year	
Academic				
Study methods	256	(44%)	169	(49%)
Handling content of courses	191	(33%)	63	(18%)**
Time	360	(62%)	131	(38%)**
Extracurricular				
Generally getting acquainted with				
Harvard	90	(16%)	36	(10%)
Learning to live on your own	67	(12%)	24	(7%)*
Being in a city like Boston	18	(3%)	8	(2%)
Interpersonal				
Dormitory life	38	(7%)	32	(9%)
Getting acquainted with students	61	(11%)	68	(20%)**
Getting acquainted with faculty	83	(14%)	136	(39%)**
Meeting girls	74	(13%)	115	(33%)**
Getting into extracurricular activities	48	(8%)	37	(11%)
	N = 579		N = 347	

Note: *Difference between freshman and senior year is significant by chi square at < .05
**Difference between freshman and senior year is significant by chi square at < .01

level for a particular person and the kind of variation around that level.

Certain developmental or maturational stages play a particularly important role in shaping self-esteem. In the earliest years, it is probably dependent on a trusting and supportive relationship with the mother and other members of the family—in Jellinec's case, his mother and older brothers. Abused infants and children appear to be hypervigilant, shy, and sensitive, whereas those from warm and caring families are more likely to be secure and outgoing; the characteristics occur with low and high self-esteem, respectively. In the developmental sequence, the first real challenge to self-esteem may come with the school experience. Not only does the child have direct competition with peers, but the immediate support of the parents is lacking. Some, of course, thrive on the new-found freedom.

Adolescence is likely to be the next phase in which there is a challenge to self-esteem. These are years of physical change, of altered internal states, and of shifts in social expectations and rewards, all of which may make it difficult for an individual to keep self-esteem high. Even those for whom adolescence goes smoothly often report that self-doubts plagued them at times and that they went all too easily from high regard to doubt. For many adolescents, the settling of this issue on the positive side is an event dearly wished for.

Admission to college can at first elevate self-esteem, particularly if the student is accepted by a college high on his list of choices. Then, if the atmosphere is highly competitive, the student may be confronted by a new challenge, as Jason was in his Slavic course. Almost everyone needs some external evidence, some rewards, for building self-esteem or holding it up. The freshman, relying mainly on his previous academic record, soon realizes that he will be measured by different standards in college. It takes time for many students to build up a backlog of evidence that they can do acceptable work. In the early sixties, our students referred to this as "learning to cut the mustard." For students living away from home it may be particularly fateful, because there is no family to fall back on. Depressions in the freshman and even the sophomore year are often related to the resulting self-doubt.

The challenge in the environment also has the potential for raising self-esteem. By altering home ties, a student has the opportunity to make more decisions for himself, especially if he attends a college that encourages freedom. Becoming adept at making these decisions can lead to a sense of autonomy and power, which in turn may result in an increase of self-esteem. The whole process is aided by the increase in knowledge and the sharpening of skills that are the usual fruits of college. If all goes well, the student finds out, if he has doubted before, that he is good for something, that he has negotiable talent, and thus may feel more secure in his self-regard. Because he did high honors work, Jellinec found that he had intellectual talents that were real and not fancied.

Apart from academic factors, the environment/person interaction is important in other ways. During the span of time covered by the adolescent and young adult years, our society grants more of the symbols and prerogatives of adult status, sometimes by legal changes or admission to new roles and sometimes by altered social expectations. These changes do not occur all at once and often are in conflict with each other; in the adolescent years they can easily cause confusion and frustration. But by the time of college, there is a clearer move toward granting the student an adult status, especially in institutions that allow a great deal of freedom. Harvard, for example, encourages students from the beginning to make their own decisions about courses, attending classes, participating in extracurricular activities, and the extent to which they wish to become involved in college life.

Over this span of years the environment can affect self-esteem first in a negative way, by not making clear a person's status in the society, and later in a positive way, by more definitive granting of adult status. Some people are quite dependent on the environment for their self-regard, often from early childhood, and get thrown easily by inconsistent expectations or, in the academic area, by poor grades on examinations. Others, like Jellinec, seem to have an inner assurance of living up to their ambitions and goals. In our studies we paid close attention to both aspects, even though the emphasis thus far has been on environmental influences.

One of the growth tasks of adolescence and young adulthood is the stabilization of self-esteem, acquiring the ability to right oneself when shaken by some negative environmental event. Some people appear to have built-in ways of regaining their equilibrium, others learn it through experience, and some never seem to achieve that quality. Being able to regain equilibrium is itself an adaptive move in an autoplastic sense, that is, in terms of efficiency, but it also means that the person is better able to deal with problems in the environment. This is alloplastic adaptation, or effectiveness. There are various strategies a person can use to recover equilibrium, but we will defer their description until later, letting them arise out of other case material.

Interests

Although college admissions committees consider an applicant's interests to be important criteria in selection, these interests have often been underrated by psychologists and psychoanalysts as important in both personality growth and adaptation. There are exceptions. In his *Lives in Progress,* Robert White[3] emphasizes the deepening of interests as an important growth trend between adolescence and adulthood. He bases his formulation on John Dewey's definition of an interest as connected with an activity that engages a person in wholehearted fashion, illustrated by Jellinec's involvement with sports. White states that the important quality is absorption in the object of interest and a closer identification of one's abilities with that object. In this regard, he appears to have drawn on the writings of his colleague and teacher, Henry Murray, who described interests in terms of cathection to an object. Here, of course, Murray drew on Freud's idea of cathexis and the capacity of an object (human or otherwise) to arouse a need in a person.

White says that deepening of interests, or absorption, does not necessarily refer to the amount of time spent, but represents a state in which there is a sense of reward from doing something for its own sake. Deepening occurs as there are satisfying transactions with the objects of the interest. A person becomes more alert to the various facets and subtleties of the object of interest and feels a greater sense of reward in dealing with the object.

For our purposes, we defined an interest as a readily indentifiable, relatively constant configuration of attitudes and behavior toward a person, idea and/or physical objects that fulfills needs as these are integrated with the demands of reality, with superego requirements, and with the abilities of the person. An interest can be relatively autonomous from drives (used in the psychoanalytic sense), defenses, and social forces, but when it is dominant and per-

3. Robert W. White, *Lives in Progress,* 2nd. ed. (New York: Holt, Rinehart and Winston, 1966).

sistent it can gratify instinctual tendencies, utilize skills, and be directed toward highly cathected objects.

Interests represent a fusion of abilities and experience and, in the case of the latter, are often motivated by factors that go back to early childhood, as in the support given to Jellinec by his older brothers in baseball. Sex role differentiation by parents and other members of the child's social group leads very early to the designation of broad classes of interests that are appropriate or "legitimate" for the child and others that are not. Narrower classes of potential interests will be defined by activities pursued by parents and by the child's subcultural reference group. The physical surroundings and economic situation in which the child is reared also limit or expand interest possibilities. This social context of interest development can be called the *opportunity structure,* something that influences the development and continuation of interests throughout the life cycle. To illustrate, from a different case, we might consider a boy born and reared in a small town in Idaho, close by the streams and rivers where the steelhead run, near the mountains where deer and elk can be hunted in the fall. His family was oriented toward the soil and to occupations involving physical rather than intellectual activity. Although his mother had been a schoolteacher and there were books in the home, the family activities and those of his friends took him outside, and his early memories were of camping trips, his father fishing, and his own struggles to shoot a bow and arrow. In contrast, one of his classmates was born and reared in a borough of New York City, close by the subway and only a few nickels away from the stores, museums, and bright lights of downtown Manhattan. His family, in paternal occupation and in common activities, were oriented toward ideas, intellectual operations, and interactions with people in the neighborhood. He had little opportunity to wander outside the house unescorted, to explore the physical world, and his early memories were of heated discussions in the kitchen between his father and his uncles, with laughter as well as anger, and of his struggles with words and pictures in books long before he was ready for school.

The differences may appear contrived, though in fact we had two such students in our sample. The differences may also appear ob-

vious, though in fact such varied opportunity structures in the
origin of interests are often overlooked. As shown already in
the case of Jason Jellinec, the different careers each of our subjects pursued at Harvard can be explained in part by these experiences in early childhood and later school years.

Though many interests find their beginnings early in life and
thus illustrate the theme of continuity to later years, others come
on only as cognitive and emotional development reach certain
levels of maturity. Interests that involve a higher order of conceptual operations must await the ability for abstract thinking, which
only reaches maturity for most individuals in adolescence. Thus
the secondary school years hold an important place in the
development of interests because boys and girls often find new
powers at that time which are encouraged by the school curricu-
lum and often by extracurricular activities and the peer group.
Some students find interests that carry through college and on
into an occupation or to life-long avocations.

By the time of college, it would appear that much is set for the
individual, that his interests are fairly well determined. This is at
least partly true in terms of general orientations and of certain
specific interests. Jellinec's unchanging interest in occupations
that involved working with people is a case in point. It is also
more likely to be true if the student selects a college that
replicates much of his previous cultural and intellectual experience. Grinker[4] noted such continuation in his study of students at
George Williams College.

Often, however, college provides occasion for another expansion
and alteration of interests, given sufficient but not extreme contrast with previous experience and given freedom and encouragement
for exploration. To use our earlier term, the opportunity structure
of a given college may have a significant effect on the development
of new interests or on the consolidation of earlier interests through
confrontation with different possibilities. In colleges that offer a
rich diversity of activities, there are opportunities to take courses
in areas not pursued before, to enter into extracurricular activities
not possible previously, or to hear about ideas or experiences from

4. Roy R. Grinker, " 'Mentally Healthy' Young Males (Homoclites)," *Archives of General Psychiatry*, 6 (June 1962), 405–453.

peers and adults that are very different from the person's past experience. Two illustrations will suffice.

In the early sixties two popular courses at Harvard were Music I and Fine Arts 13. The latter was known as "Darkness at Noon," apparently because it was held from twelve to one and the lights were always turned off for slides of paintings and architecture. Some students knew little about classical music or fine arts and found in these courses, for which there was peer group support, new vistas of experience, as Jellinec did with the Boston Symphony in his freshman year.

Harvard is within easy driving distance of some major ski slopes, and many students took weekends or vacations for this sport. There were always two or three second-hand hearses parked around the Houses, which had been converted to sleeping and eating accommodations and provided unusual as well as practical transportation for ski trips. Other students, especially those reared in the South, had had no previous experience with the sport, but more than one of them in our sample learned to ski while at Harvard and derived a great deal of enjoyment from it.

The big advantage of the college years is again the moratorium, the chance to try different ideas or interests without the kind of commitment that might be dictated later by time demands of a job or of family responsibilities. Not only does a moratorium allow time, but it also sanctions trial and error behavior and encourages a student to sample things as part of the educational process. Colleges, of course, differ in the degree allowed a moratorium. A six-year program leading to a combination of the A.B. and M.D. degrees or an engineering institute is less open or flexible for new interests than a liberal arts college with a tradition for educating a well-rounded person who can defer his specialization until graduate school.

As a first step in considering the relationship of interests to the process of adaptation, it is important to remember that there can be self-directed and object-person-directed interests. Those directed toward the self may be in the service of self-preservation, of self-aggrandizement (as for prestige or power), or of self-advantage (as for wealth). Sometimes self-directed interests lead to greater efficiency and thus enable the person to be more successful in that aspect of adaptation. This is particularly true if external pressures

are severe or hostile or if the person has been limited in the development of good object relationships. Under other conditions, the narcissistic quality of interests can restrict emotional income and can interfere with adaptation to external demands, particularly if these demands are reasonable rather than severe.

Outwardly directed or object-centered interests can have a number of aims, one of which is self-advantage. This is different from a self-directed interest, for the cathexis is in an object, even though the person may gain materially or socially from pursuing the interest. There can also be altruistic aims, where the advantage is for others, or aims of mutual benefit, for both self and others. Sometimes object-directed interests can lead to greater effectiveness in adaptation, particularly if the interests serve the social group well and there are appropriate rewards, tangible or intangible, for the individual. The danger lies in an overinvestment in object-centered interests, which might leave the person vulnerable if the interests were cut off suddenly, as with crippling disease or injury. Jason Jellinec learned at Harvard that he would not be bereft should opportunity for sports be limited.

Interests that have mutual benefits to a number of people are important in adaptation because they provide a way of binding people together and thus serve needs for group support. Recreational interests are good illustrations, whether in the form of team participation or of common spectator interest. We found that in a number of our subjects recreational interests were important factors in holding roommate groups together, and not necessarily because they were all athletes themselves. Much of the energy directed toward sports in the early sixties may now be going into social and political activities, but the same adaptive purposes can be served in protest movements as in sports.

Finally, interests can be in the service of adaptation when they provide for the mutual expression of such factors within the individual as needs and drives, skills, and superego dictates in the form of values and standards. Mutual expression suggests that conflict among these factors is absent or is at least limited in scope. Interests associated with occupational plans can have that integrative function, although other kinds of interests can, too. One of our students, a biology concentrator, spent his summers working for a government agency concerned with wildlife management. Part of his job was tagging and accumulating movement data about deer. He had strong needs for physical activity, which could be satisfied, and for autonomy, which were fulfilled because much of the work had to be done on his own. Even in those days of the early sixties, he was an "ecology nut," which is to say that he hated waste and destruction and wanted to preserve the natural order. He placed value on the preservation of life. His interest led to the writing of an honors thesis on animal ecology and to a decision on medicine as a career. In the latter he could satisfy his high technical skills, his needs, and his values for life.

In presenting the material on Jellinec, we talked about interests, values, and goals together, as one characteristic of his personality. Subsequently, it became apparent that a finer discrimination needed to be made, and that is reflected here in the distinction between interests and goals.

Goal-Directed Behavior

Goals refer to future states or conditions, either immediate or long-range, toward which the person strives. They help to mobilize and direct energies into particular channels and hence have motivational characteristics. They act as guidelines or selectors, enabling a person to inhibit some courses of action in favor of others. They have a hierarchical quality, giving priority to some actions over others when there is a range of possible actions or when the environment presents limited alternatives. In this sense, goals act as ordering mechanisms.

Although goals have something in common with interests, they are different both in future orientation and also in their tendencies to represent values. Values are consciously held standards by which we measure for ourselves the desirable and undesirable, the important and unimportant, and the right and wrong. They tell us how to choose between objects and events. Goals and values have been much in the center of the changes taking place in the last decade, and it is on these issues that some of the younger generation say their lives will depart from those of their elders. Many of the alterations in goals can be better understood through the scheme of values that was originally presented by Florence Kluckhohn.[5]

There are a limited number of questions about human existence for which every social group must find some solution. Kluckhohn develops her scheme around five questions: what is the innate predisposition of man, what is the kind of relationship between man and nature, what is the significant time dimension, what personality type is most valued, and what is the dominant modality of the relationship between men? There are a limited number of answers for each question, and the particular answers that any social group works out will affect the goals of a person within that group.

The question about the predisposition of man can be answered by one of three categories. Man may be viewed as inherently evil, as in the doctrine of original sin, or as basically neither evil nor good, or as essentially good. On the question of man's relation to nature, man can be viewed as subjugated to nature, as part of nature in a harmonious whole, or as sovereign over nature, harnessing its forces for his own ends. The latter orientation has been characteristic of American society, the outcome of the application of the scientific method. A growing interest among the young in such diverse topics as ecology and astrology suggest that alternative views are being considered.

Answers to the question about time orientation refer, of course, to the past, present, and future. Our society has been characterized by a future-oriented, time-conscious position, which regards delay of gratification as worthwhile and emphasizes commitment to long-term goals. Certain aspects of contemporary youth culture emphasize greater concern with the present, which suggests that a fundamental shift may be taking place in values, although the degree of present time orientation that will become permanent is not yet clear.

The valued personality type concerns the way a person uses his energies and the sources of his satisfactions. Kluckhohn defines three categories as possible answers: the being, the being-in-becoming, and the doing. The first stresses spontaneity, the second stress-

5. Florence R. Kluckhohn, "Dominant and Variant Value Orientations," in Clyde Kluckhohn, Henry A. Murray, and David M. Schneider (eds.), *Personality in Nature, Society, and Culture,* 2nd ed. (New York: Alfred A. Knopf, 1955), pp. 342–357.

es self-development and self-realization, and the third is distinguished by its demand for action and accomplishments according to standards external to the individual. Again, this is an area where there may be a shift in the present day from a doing orientation to either being or being-in-becoming.

Finally, in the interrelationship among men, Kluckhohn distinguishes three categories: the lineal, which emphasizes the continuity of the group through time; the collateral, which focuses on one's family or close associates at a given point in time; and the individualistic, where individual goals have primacy over those of the group at any point in time. Although the last of these has been generally characteristic of American culture, some people today are calling for social organizations, like the communes, that stress collaterality.

Not only do goals exemplify value orientations; they also act as important organizing factors within the personality, especially with reference to interests. Thus, goals may encourage the expression of some interests while denying or postponing the expression of others. The student who wants to become a physician may put aside an abiding interest in music and leave his piano untouched for years in order to give the necessary time to his medical training. He may never return to it, or else he may pick it up again when his days as a house officer are over.

Goals also give meaning to disparate kinds of behavior. The sense of purpose often associated with goal-directed activity may enable a person to endure psychic or physical pain without damaging effects and to hew to a stable course in spite of frustrating setbacks. Jason's statement that he would do anything to keep from flunking out of Harvard is one illustration of this.

In the young child, goals are limited because his experience is limited and because his cognitive organization has not advanced far enough for him to think too far into the future. Goals at that period are mostly short-range and are mostly related to pleasurable activities based on the gratification of physical impulses. Very quickly, however, the effect of the family and others in the social group begins to shape goals by the proscriptions and allowances given for various behaviors. The child learns what his parents consider to be right and desirable and to make these responses part of his own repertoire. This is the matrix of his value system and of his goal-oriented behavior.

The social group, and especially the family, if he is part of one, continue to be the crucial factors in the development of new goals. As cognitive apparatus becomes more differentiated, the possibility of future-oriented behavior is enhanced, and if the social group stresses the importance of future events, the child may develop the capacity for planning his actions in anticipation of future states. By the time the child is ten or twelve this capacity is well established.

Adolescence offers the possibility of further development of goal behavior because there is often a merging of values with the growing sense of personal power and future autonomy that many adolescents feel. There is often a stretching for ideals, particularly about what the person may be able to do to right some of the wrongs of society or to bring in new experiences for himself and others. The idealism may take a number of forms. One is immediate action, like taking part in political movements to bring about change in school, municipal, or even national affairs, or to combat problems like pollution, voter apathy, deteriorating neighborhoods, or social inequity, as Jason did with tutoring. Here the goal is primarily social and the individual merges himself in a larger cause.

In another form, the person may decide on a future career that expresses his ideals, perhaps through medicine or nursing, or teaching, or the clergy, and through courses, college planning, and other activities may point himself in that direction. His view of the occupation is likely to stress the most desirable aspects, but that can be a powerful motivator.

These idealistic anticipations of the future we have come to call "great expectations," to indicate that the anticipations may be larger than reality, greater than the person can fulfill. This may be particularly true as the high school senior anticipates college and the life he will lead there. One of our subjects, Jonathan Thackery, recalled his fantasies about coming to Harvard in the following manner:

> As I remember, I was quite sure that I would spend practically every . . . it's what I still think Oxford must be like . . . or Oxford a hundred years ago . . . I expected that every, or practically every day, I would be sitting in the common room, and everyone wearing tweeds, and we'd be talking about great things for an hour or so. And I would be reading, but not in the

sense of reading for an exam. But I'd be reading and writing poetry, and would study very hard, and make straight A's, because this is the place where only the academic is considered important. It would be in a way a small community, and we'd all know such-and-such. And we'd have lots of intramural contests and a great many dinners. I don't know . . . I thought it would be like Oxford. Well, it wasn't that way at all.

I thought that I'd probably enter campus politics. There's nothing of that sort here. I thought I would join the literary magazine right away and there'd be a very flourishing literary activity and we'd all create and write. That didn't happen.

This quality of stretching for ideals does not happen to all adolescents, probably only to those whose social and economic circumstances provide the possibility of acting upon the environment in the way we have described, probably only to those who have been reared in families where the values encourage individual initiative and social concern, and probably only to those who have sufficient self-esteem and sense of power to lend credence to their dreams of glory. Among the group we studied, however, "great expectations" were not uncommon.

The interaction between student and college brings some reality-testing to idealism, but it also offers the student the possibility of changing and altering goals. Many colleges encourage students to question and rethink their value system; they are challenged in this by courses and by arguments with their peers. An occasional outcome of that questioning is a major shift in life goals. Perhaps there have been more instances of this in the late sixties than in the previous few decades. A more likely outcome is an alteration of goals rather than a breaking away, much as we described earlier in our presentation of the continuity model of development. That can occur not only through a rethinking of values, but also through a widened understanding of potential activities in which the person might become involved. For many students, college opens doors into careers or actions that they knew about before.

Goal-directed behavior that is attainable and realistically based, rather than resting on fantasy or wish, is particularly sensitive to what is happening in the environment, perhaps more sensitive than any of the other variables presented here. We emphasize that fact because the current social change involves a possible change in the values that are generally characteristic of our society. When our students matriculated, the change was only beginning, but the succeeding years have seen a quickening pace. As yet, we do not have enough historical perspective to cite trends or describe the shape of a new value system. But for many students at the present time, going to college may facilitate some important change in their goals.

Adaptation is aided by goal-directed behavior through its motivational and organizing features. Clearly defined goals can serve efficiency within the personality through reducing conflicts, providing outlets for impulse expression, and enhancing self-esteem. The goalless person has a difficult time adapting because he is so much at the mercy of events around him.

Goals also are important in alloplastic adaptation, particularly when the behavior is directed toward social ends, as in political behavior or any of the service occupations. Goals are not just occupational in nature, however, and many kinds of life-style goals can have an important effect on the environment.

Mood

Jason Jellinec was a person who was relatively even in mood and who had relatively infrequent depressed states. We noted that there was little change in his mood over the four years. But, as we studied other students, we found more variability and were impressed by the fact that it is a central variable in the college years.

A pervasive emotional state, an ego state, in which an emotion or set of emotions gains ascendency and which is strong enough to affect a person's perception of events and his behavior toward people and things, is the common definition of *mood*. Though pervasive, mood normally has a limited quality in terms of time; that is, moods change, they come and go and respond to shifts in environmental experience. Common usage refers to being in a "good mood" or "bad mood," the former denoting a happy or humorous state, the latter, one that is depressed or petulant. When we speak of a person as being moody, common usage emphasizes the possible pathology involved; that is, the person is given to fits of depression or bad temper. Mood, however, should refer to a variety of emotional states—humorous, joyous, despairing, or peevish.

Mood can be distinguished from temperament, which Webster[6] defines as the peculiar physical and mental character of an individual. Temperament refers to personality types, which may be associated with body build or somatotypes, as in the scheme put forth by W. H. Sheldon.[7] Since the days of the Greek philosophers, there has been reference to the sanguine, phlegmatic, choleric, and melancholic temperaments, formerly attributed to different humors or physical substrates. Mood and temperament are related phenomena because mood reflects an underlying temperament that must be considered in understanding a particular mood. Temperament, however, is little influenced by the environment, whereas mood reflects to a certain degree what is transpiring in the environment.

Two aspects of mood are important in our case studies; one is that of level, and the other of variability. The former refers to how happy or unhappy, how calm or irritable a person is at a given time. By taking repeated measurements over time or by making ratings of how a person feels, some indication of the average level of various emotional states can be made. Thus, some students might be characterized as generally unhappy and others as generally happy; Jellinec was generally happy. Variability refers to the frequency with which mood shifts occur and the degree to which mood swings depart from a base or average level. In any measurement of variability, one must take into account the events transpiring in the environment, because the frequency of occurrence of such things as rewards or punishments can influence swings of mood. Over the four years of college, we were interested in the extent to which there was change in dominant mood or in range of moods and also in the extent to which a change had occurred in stabilization, that is, in the control of the frequency and degree of mood swings.

From a developmental point of view, we must consider the possibilities that mood level and variability are both dependent on biochemical and central nervous system factors and that an innate predisposition toward mood reactivity may be present. A particular

6. *Webster's New Collegiate Dictionary* (Springfield, Mass.: G. and C. Merriam Co., 1953).

7. W. H. Sheldon, S. S. Stevens, and W. B. Tucker, *The Varieties of Human Physique* (New York: Harper, 1940).

person's constitutional endowment might make him more likely to be a happy person, for whom fairly disturbing environmental factors would be necessary to bring about a depression. Another person might be the opposite, one for whom constant assurance from others would be necessary to keep his moods away from depression. At the moment we can only speculate about these possibilities, not prove them, yet an understanding of mood level and variability must consider them.

Even if one grants a constitutional factor in mood, the importance of early development in the family and continuing effect of the environment cannot be discounted. The young child soon learns how his parents react to events, whether they take disturbing information with equanimity, whether they become depressed at slights from others, whether they get grouchy when frustrated. Many of these cues he will adopt for his own behavior, in the process of imitation, and thus follow parental style. Of course, he does not take over parental reaction patterns completely, but he is likely to react in ways somewhat similar to those of his parents. Mood level and variability in the child are more likely to reflect patterns in the immediate family than those in the wider social group. Here is where there is a subtle difference between mood and our other variables, like interests.

In the developmental sequence, patterns of mood behavior are likely to change during adolescence because that life phase is one in which there are significant hormonal changes, in which the person is quite conscious of an altered body state, and in which there is a shift in the perceptions and expectations of others toward the adolescent. Quite often, the degree of mood swings becomes exaggerated from previous behavior; that is, the downswings are toward deeper depression, and the upswings are toward an ecstatic state of rapture and joy. The intensity of feeling in the adolescent may be very strong. At the same time, shift in moods often comes quickly. At one moment the person may be very happy and only a little later be depressed, with little indication to an observer of why the shift has taken place. Parents often report that they are puzzled and frustrated by these sudden shifts because they cannot understand why they occur and find themselves constantly adjusting to varying states of their offspring. The adolescent himself may be distressed by the shifts because they do not seem to be fully under his control.

Mood and the variations on it become very important in the process of adaptation. When a person is happy, or in a good mood, he is more likely to be open to stimuli and to use exploratory activity, to become engaged with the environment. He is more likely to consider various alternatives for action. Under these circumstances, the possibilities for all kinds of learning are enhanced. Course work in college is more likely to be exciting and more productive. Some students report a drop-off in grades when they are depressed, as in the sophomore slump, and a noticeable improvement in academic performance when the depression passes.

One characteristic of a depressed mood is the reduction in response to stimuli because the person turns his attention much more in upon himself. He "sees" and "hears" fewer things; only those that are self-related become important, and then as negative rather than positive possibilities. Depressed persons are usually less motivated to overt activity and have less engagement with their surroundings. In the fall term of his junior year, Jason reported that he had difficulty studying and was annoying to his roommates, a mood of depression related to his loss of Nancy.

Lest the previous paragraph sound as though depression is always equated with pathology, it should be noted that a certain amount of depression may be constructive or adaptive at times. Under its effects a person may become more sensitive to others, and it may go along with the development of a kind of social consciousness, a *Weltschmerz*. Perhaps, as with anxiety, there may be a certain optimal level of depression that is constructive.

Both extremes of mood—elation and depression—can interfere with adaptation and can become life-threatening. An individual in a manic state has trouble stopping the inflow of stimuli and consequently shifts rapidly from one topic to another, cannot concentrate on a topic, and often makes serious errors in judgment. He may so misjudge events as to put himself in a most vulnerable position, physically or psychologically. In severe depression, the withdrawal from stimuli can lead to almost complete inactivity and of course to suicidal behavior. These extremes, however, occur in only a small proportion of people and only on certain occasions.

They were not to be expected among our subjects, but they are vivid illustrations of the close relationship between mood and the adaptational process.

With particular reference to the autoplastic aspect of adaptation, mood affects feedback loops, so that under conditions of happiness, positive loops that enhance self-esteem are set in motion, whereas in depression, negative loops that contribute to lowered self-esteem occur.

Specific information about mood in college students can be found in a recent study of students at Radcliffe and Harvard by Alden Wessman and David Ricks.[8] Each subject made self-ratings on mood for a six-week period, and the Harvard students were given a battery of psychological tests. Over the span of the study, students differed from each other in *average mood level;* that is, some were more happy, others generally less so. There were also individual differences in *stability of mood;* some were rather constant, others fluctuated a good deal. The authors found that the dimension of happiness-unhappiness was the most crucial and was broadly indicative of all of one's affective experiences.

The most important findings for our study were of two kinds. First, the stable men tended to make fine distinctions in their feelings; the moody men did not. From this, Wessman and Ricks concluded that the stable men appeared to have more complexity and differentiation in their affective lives. Second, when situations of low mood and high mood were compared for all students, the data showed that in low moods ideal and actual self were farther apart, self-concept was less favorable, and subjects were more irritable, more likely to blame others for their troubles, and not as likely to persist in activities.

Control

One of the notable aspects of Jason Jellinec's personality was his ego control and his use of coping mechanisms, the major reasons for his ability to make the shift from the Great Plains to Cambridge. A number of different facets to ego control emerged, however, as

8. Alden E. Wessman and David F. Ricks, *Mood and Personality* (New York: Holt, Rinehart and Winston, 1966).

we studied more case histories. For our use, we have three aspects in mind: control as restraint or inhibition of impulses, as the directing and guiding of cognitive, emotional, and/or motor responses, and as management of tension. It is not easy to discuss these aspects without being caught up in value judgments, especially when talking about inhibition and restraint, but we will consider the *process* rather than the forms of control. Ways of impulse gratification vary from one person to another, and guidelines for restraint vary from one cultural group to another, but in each case an ego function is at work and that function can be studied in terms of development and its relationship to adaptation.

Our assumption is that the basic initiators of action are biological factors that come to have mental associations and elaborations, and that as development proceeds, the mental elaborations can become direct initiators in themselves. In some psychological theories, these biological factors are called drives. Much of the process of parent-child interaction or group-child interaction is given to putting some kind of restraint or control on the direct and free expression of the basic drives and the elaborated needs. The mores and customs of a cultural group, as well as the laws of the state, continue to serve in later years as restraining influences on the expression of impulses and drives. For example, all societies have customs that indicate at what time and with whom sexual intercourse may occur, although these customs vary greatly across the world. Many of the customs are stated in laws, as in regard to sexual relations with minors, or definitions of adultery, or restrictions on prostitution or homosexuality. A similar situation exists for the aggressive drive; our society, for example, has a complicated system of both civil and criminal law that handles assault and injury.

No society is so primitive that it does not have some patterns of restraint, although the degree of permissiveness or restriction varies widely from one society to another. By and large, any child is taught some form of restraint in certain areas. As he is reared, the context for a pattern of restraint comes both from the customs and laws of his society and from the particular accommodation to those customs and laws that has been reached by his family group. In times of social stability and consensus, of high social integration, variation from the social norms will be relatively slight. When social change occurs and there is fragmentation and questioning of norms, family variation in standards of control will be greater. We would expect any entering class at college, particularly when students come from a diversity of cultural backgrounds, to display individual differences in the type of controls on impulses as well as in the ways in which the controls are used, that is, in their consistency of use.

Individual differences in control will be due not only to early background experiences, but also to the effect of the developmental phase of adolescence through which the student has been, and may still be, passing. The physical changes of adolescence—hormonal and musculoskeletal—have a profound effect on drives in a way that represents a marked change from earlier years. The problem of finding expression for impulses in an appropriate manner or, stated negatively, of curbing impulse expression, is a major difficulty of the adolescent years for many individuals. Solution to the problem is affected both by the strength of the drives and by the strength of control mechanisms already internalized, as well as by the options available in the environment. Some adolescents go through a good deal of turmoil over impulse expression; others either do not feel particularly pressured or have adequate outlets. As a result, some students come to college anxious to be rid of a restrictive atmosphere and conflict, some with guilt and doubts about themselves, some with a balanced solution between impulses and restrictions, and some with strict and well-internalized control systems.

The college environment and interaction between college and student may have a direct effect on subsequent development of control mechanisms. Among the factors to be considered is the extent to which the college provides continuity in customs and mores with those previously encountered by the student, as some of the smaller, church-related schools seem to do, or the extent to which the college encourages the student to rethink his values and gives a wide latitude in terms of defining what is acceptable behavior.

One further point should be made about alteration in control during the college years. For some individuals, a period of relaxation of restraint may be necessary as a prelude to the reorganizing of control mechanisms. Part of the folklore of college life pictures these years as a time to sow wild oats or kick up one's heels—a "boys will be boys" attitude. Jason was so tempted at the beginning of his junior year, yet fearful he would be corrupted. After this period, the person has been expected to settle down and exercise more restraint. Implicit in all this is the idea of a lessening and then reorganization of controls. The pattern may not be as prevalent today; in fact, many students react against the party-going, devil-may-care attitude of earlier students. Yet it may be that the loosening process takes other forms, perhaps more inwardly oriented than "party" oriented. For some students, the use of psychoactive drugs may serve that purpose, not only through the effect of the drug, but also through the symbolic significance of drug-taking as a rejection of adult patterns of behavior. We do know that some students give up or restrict the use of psychoactive drugs after a while; such change may be associated with a reorganization of control.

The second aspect of control differs subtly from the first because the emphasis is not on restriction or limitation, but on directing or guiding. Even though restriction has a rational or conscious aspect, the utilization of intellectual or cognitive processes is more marked in the guiding function. Mastery of knowledge of various aspects of the world is necessary to the gaining of control. On that basis, the person can anticipate and plan, can judge how his actions will affect things, can tell what is likely to be successful or unsuccessful. The cognitive process involved is *experimental thinking,* which is abstract rather than concrete because alternative actions and their implications are considered in the mind without recourse to physical action and often without incoming sensory stimuli. To be able to think experimentally, a person needs accumulated knowledge, either through direct experience or through teaching, as in a classroom, together with the neurological maturation that allows for abstract thought. All people do not have the capacity for abstract thought to the same degree. The spectrum is wide, but in college we deal with indviduals who are more likely to be proficient in it. Within the last few decades, the developmental stages of abstract thinking have been mapped, first by Jean Piaget and more recently by Jerome Bruner and his associates.[9] The last developmental refinement seems to occur by adolescence, meaning that full abstract thinking in most individuals is not possible until that life phase.

College or university experience, particularly in the classroom,

9. Jean Piaget, *Judgment and Reasoning in the Child* (New York: Harcourt, Brace, 1928); Jerome S. Bruner et al., *Studies in Cognitive Growth* (New York: John Wiley and Sons, 1966).

has the potential for increasing intellectual mastery by adding to the student's amount of knowledge (the acquisition of facts) and by giving him greater opportunities for experimental thinking. Most college teachers encourage their students to weigh alternatives, to consider all the possibilities that might be present in a given set of facts, and to compare the relative dominance of various conclusions. This certainly is the tradition at Harvard, and the typical examination question in the humanities or social sciences will ask the student to describe and discuss broad issues. The process of arriving at a conclusion is often given as much weight in grading as the conclusion itself. In order to write a good examination, the student must learn to shift from "black-and-white" thinking to "shades-of-gray" thinking; that is, from dichotomous, either-or evaluation to a consideration of the manner in which things fit together as the circumstances are varied.[10] Jellinec had particular difficulty with this in his freshman year and could not follow from one item to another in a logical manner, but he learned to do so before he graduated.

With intellectual mastery should come a heightened ability to control one's future, to redirect impulses, to control the actions of others, and to manage the environment. With the latter two aspects, we can speak of the control as alloplastic, where a person shapes his world in terms of both people and things. Circumstances as well as individual ability, of course, will determine how successful this will be.

A caution is also in order to the reader, for it is easy to place value judgments on the control of others, to view the process in terms of certain extremes, such as the Machiavellian approach to control. We submit that in the process of adaptation some kind of control over the environment, including other people, is necessary, and that an important part of the process of personality development is to learn about the capacity and the responsibilities in that control. Social customs and laws aid the individual in determining how he will use his energies to that end, but college provides an opportunity to think through the issues involved and

10. For an interesting and provocative study of changes in cognitive style among Harvard students, see William H. Perry, Jr., *Forms of Intellectual and Ethical Development in the College Years* (New York: Holt, Rinehart and Winston, 1968).

to test out cognitive skills in exercising increased environmental control.

Management of tension, the third aspect of control, refers to the control of such factors as pain, anxiety, threat, and disturbing information, which might upset or make it difficult for the person to keep within the normal limits of homeostatic balance. The task is to keep the tension down. It is characteristic of life that people are threatened periodically, although the seriousness and the frequency of the threats vary. Some persons are able to lead quite protected lives, whereas others always seem to be in situations of deprivation or danger. We also must remember that threats can be internal as well as external, from biological malfunctioning or from the psychic representations of possible external threats. Our main consideration, however, is with the handling of physical pain or painful affect, whether the latter arises from internal or external sources.

The manner in which a person controls or handles painful affect has been dealt with at considerable length in the psychological literature. Much of psychoanalytic writing, for example, has described the utilization of ego defense mechanisms, such as repression, projection, denial, reaction formation, and others. Freud dealt with the issue as a central one in his work, and the system of defense mechanisms has been elaborated by psychoanalytic writers who have followed him. When the defenses are used in a rigid, repetitive way or on unconscious, irrational grounds, we can say that they serve neurotic purposes. But they also are used by all people in one form or another at various times to control painful affect. That fact has led some recent investigators[11] to differentiate between defense and coping mechanisms, reserving the latter for those that are more flexible, reality-oriented, and conscious. Logical analysis, empathy, tolerance of ambiguity, and sublimation are examples of coping mechanisms. For our purposes, both defense and coping mechanisms are means of control or management of tension.

11. Theodore C. Kroeber, "The Coping Functions of the Ego Mechanisms," in Robert W. White (ed.), *The Study of Lives* (New York: Atherton Press, 1963), pp. 178-198, Norma Haan, "Coping and Defense Mechanisms Related to Personality Inventories," *Journal of Consulting Psychology*, 29 (August 1965), 373-378, and "Proposed Model of Ego Functioning: Coping and Defense Mechanisms in Relationship to IQ Change," *Psychological Monographs*, 77 (1963), 1-23.

Lest the reader assume we mean that control should equal elimination of painful affect, we point out that at times control may involve the constructive, anticipatory use of anger or anxiety. The paradigm for such use is the "work of worrying," as in Irving Janis's[12] study of pre- and postoperative reactions of surgical patients. Those with moderate anticipatory anxiety had a better postoperative outcome than patients who reported little or no anxiety or those who were very much afraid. In such circumstances, the interrelationship between the various kinds of control is apparent because the constructive use of anxiety also involves a certain amount of experimental thinking.

The basis for mechanisms used in the managment of tension comes in early life experiences through observing how they are used by others and in reacting to the kinds of controls imposed by parents and others on one's own behavior. Subsequent life experiences serve to modify the defensive structure developed in the early years, especially if the person lives in a situation of continued psychological or physical threat or has frightening or disturbing experiences without much emotional support in handling the ensuing emotional reaction. Once again, adolescence may awaken old issues that have been put out of sight by a defensive apparatus; or, because of the person's heightened sensitivity, he may need stronger controls to handle depression and unease. We have noted that adolescence can be a time of turmoil and thus of greater disturbing affect. In such cases the management of tension may be an important factor. We should note here that later life phases can also be ones where disturbing affect is high, especially through pressures from the environment, through physical changes, or experiences of loss.

The effect of college on management of tension may not be as direct as it is in the development of experimental thinking. Rather, the ability of the student to tolerate disturbing affect and at times to use it constructively is affected by his growing sense of independence from parents, and thus of autonomy, and by the imitative experience in peer interaction, by seeing his friends handle things. Certain group experiences may also be contributory. Organized athletics are sometimes derided today because of the

12. Irving L. Janis, *Psychological Stress* (New York: John Wiley and Sons, 1958).

emphasis on team and school spirit and because of the strong emphasis on competition and winning for winning's sake. Easily forgotten is the fact that team sports can be useful in management of tension through the sharing of strong feelings, through the emotional support of the group in time of crisis, and through peer pressure for individual fortitude in the face of physical or emotional pain. This was an often silent but ever-present process for Jellinec. These same qualities can come, of course, from other kinds of group activity; some students may be finding them today in political groups that are actively confronting the problems of society.

Finally, the overall effect of moving into adult status and of finding changed expectations by parents and other adult figures provides for most people a greater sense of ability to handle problems. Social and physical maturation into adulthood is not limited, of course, to the college student. Therefore, particular college experiences of the kind we have mentioned are secondary and facilitating rather than primary.

There is some merit in concluding these remarks about control by going back to the issue with which our theoretical discussion opened, that of adaptation. Each of the aspects of control that we have discussed bears directly on efficiency and effectiveness of adaptation. Unrestrained, undirected, or overwhelming impulses and affects leave a person vulnerable because human interaction is organized in its nature. Though the extent and form of organization varies, that quality is present in all social structure. Thus a person's feelings about the environment and his relations to it, as well as his overt behavior, involve some kind of control. If control is missing or is inappropriate to the situation, a person may have difficulty in surviving; so too, if it is very rigid and restrictive of the person's actions. Coming to terms with control in consciousness is a major developmental task, perhaps never completely solved by anyone, yet handled in an adequate sense by many. The college years may well be the time when the issue is most brought into awareness and the major accommodations made that will be used throughout life.

Chapter 5 / Joseph Kramer

Joseph Kramer would have had little in common with Jason Jellinec. They did not know each other at Harvard, but had they met, the acquaintance would not likely have ripened into friendship. Partly, it was a question of background, but, of more importance, their interests and goals were quite different. So too were their personality styles—the way they approached academic work, their adaptive mechanisms, and the ways they changed in college. They did not use Harvard in the same way, because for Joseph Kramer Harvard as a social institution did not loom large. He might have attended a different college and changed and developed in much the same way as he did at Harvard.

Our second case illustrates a different kind of adaptive process, a different pattern of personality changes over four years of college, and a different set of interactions between college and student. Joseph Kramer is another example of continuity between past and present, but the elements brought forward and the ways of bringing them forward are not the same as with Jason Jellinec.

Family and School Background

When Joseph arrived in Cambridge to begin his college career, he was well prepared for the experience. He had visited Harvard before when he was in the process of making college applications. He came from a relatively large city in the Midwest, had traveled

97

extensively in the United States, and had been to Europe several times. The idea of going to college had been in his mind from early years. His father was an educated man, with an advanced degree in engineering, and had made it clear to Joseph that he hoped his son would obtain a liberal education at an outstanding university. His mother echoed these sentiments, and an older sister had already graduated from a small but intellectually demanding coeducational college. The family was well-off financially through the father's success in his own manufacturing business. Other students from Joseph's high school had attended Harvard, and through conversations with them he had a picture of what life would be like.

Joseph's background had been relatively uneventful, except for incidents that transpired before his birth and affected the family tradition and ethos. Joseph's family were European Jews who, when Hitler came to power, had been forced to flee in haste, leaving money and possessions behind. They settled in the United States, and Joseph's father succeeded again in business, with the help of relatives and ties in the Jewish community that extended beyond family lines. They were more fortunate than many because no members of the family had been left behind in concentration camps. The experience, however, strengthened the cultural and religious tradition of Judaism in the family. Joseph described these events in a matter-of-fact manner, reflecting the way in which his parents regarded their experience. The father did have a somewhat old-world orientation, which, in the context of the American Midwest, seemed to accentuate his son's striving for independence.

Joseph lived in the same city all his life and in two different houses while growing up. The family was stable and close-knit, and he recalled many evenings when they would all go to the movies together or out for dinner. He did not, however, spontaneously recount rich details of family life, as Jellinec did. His school experiences were happy ones, though he was by no means a model student in the primary grades. He said that he got into a good deal of trouble, and he attributed it to having been bored because there was not enough to do. The academic and social demands of high school filled his life more fully and his energy went into accomplishments in these areas rather than the creation of trouble. The high school had a good faculty and the family never considered private school for Joseph, though he knew a few boys who came east to boarding school.

In high school he was not a member of the social club crowd, although he dated extensively and did not feel excluded from school life. He concentrated on his studies and on organization with a public service orientation. He also found an outlet for his talents and interests in organizations connected with his synagogue. Both in school and synagogue he was a leader. He gained that status from his organizational ability and his drive more than from a warmth of personality or a multitude of friends. That does not mean that he was cold or uninterested in people, rather that he was slightly aloof. In both respects he was qualitatively different from Jason. In describing these late years of secondary school, he continually emphasized his capacity for logical analysis and the manner in which he organized his life; he said less about the quality of his relationships with people. In contrast to Jason, he did not leave his heart behind when he came to Harvard. He had dated a girl steadily the previous summer but knew that when they went to their respective schools the romance would end.

As college began, Joseph had a clear opportunity for a career choice, taking a place in his father's business with the idea that eventually it would be his. In a practical way this appealed to him. The financial prospects were good. He liked the section of the country in which he had been reared. Also, he knew that it would not be many years before he had control of the business. He spoke the least about replacing his father, although we had good reason to suspect the issue was close to the surface in his mind.

Personality Structure and Harvard Experience

The activity that dominated Joseph's description of his life at Harvard was his involvement in his course work. He was not a grind in the traditional sense, because he had an extensive social life, but the major focus of his interest and the major allotment of his time was on the academic side of things. His interviews were filled with talk about grades, his study procedures, his performance on papers and examinations, and ways in which he thought he might improve his academic progress. When he talked about his instructors, he emphasized their manner of teaching, their requirements, or differences of opinion he had with them about evaluation of his work. He rarely talked about other qualities of their personalities, as Jason did in describing his relationship with his tutor. In one of his junior year interviews, Joseph Kramer had difficulty in remembering the name of his tutor.

His approach to academic work was to read all the assigned references and to attend all his classes. In addition, he audited a number of courses and went to special lectures in the late afternoon or evenings. Many students use this approach in the freshman year, but in subsequent years look for shortcuts in the readings and do not attend all the lectures. Joseph continued his initial approach throughout his four years. Also, he kept a regular study schedule rather than working in spurts or leaving the bulk of his reading until near the end of the term. He organized his days so that he could put in study time in the afternoon as well as in the evening. Further, he broke down his assigned work into units, which could then be apportioned out over the study time he had available during the week. He knew that about twenty pages an hour was his average reading speed, and he could estimate the amount of time that would be necessary to write a five-, ten-, or twenty-page paper after the reading had been finished. From this he constructed a chart that indicated the work to be done at certain times and could check off each unit on the chart as it was completed. He liked to complete a section of work for a given course before starting another topic; he said he was not comfortable in having competing tasks in his mind at the same time.

With this approach to his work, Joseph was able to keep a series of clearly defined and attainable deadlines in front of himself. He was quite aware of the value of this procedure; the deadlines kept him scared, and he said that he was most effective in getting his work done if he was scared a bit or under a certain amount of tension. He knew that he did not like to study for the joy of it and that he needed some system to force himself to do the work. Deadlines were good motives for productive work.

This type of organized activity served a number of functions for Joseph, some of which we will return to later, but one immediate adaptive function was that of meeting the academic demands of Harvard. His approach was ideal for that particular aspect of the college environment. It had a cost factor, however, in the tension

that it produced. By keeping himself on a tight schedule all
week, he felt a strong need to get away from the pressure of meeting his deadlines, and therefore a second important feature of
his college experience consisted of the things he did to relax.
This also was a conscious adaptive strategy, and he planned his
schedule so that he would have time to relax. He was an avid movie-
goer and went at least once a week, in the company of fellow students, or on a date, or often by himself. He also liked to go out
to dinner and knew most of the restaurants in the Boston area.
Both of these activities were ones that he associated with his boyhood and family life, that he had found pleasurable then, and that
now served the additional purpose of getting him away from
Harvard. Getting away became even more adaptive when Joseph
bought a car. His father had promised him one; when Joseph felt
he was settled in at Harvard, he took up his father's offer. This
meant that he could get out in the country and find restaurants
not otherwise accessible. But having a car also gave him pleasure
in the mere fact of driving, of getting away, of feeling free and on
his own. Many times when he felt tension building up, he would go
for a long drive in the country.

The moviegoing, dining out, and driving are all examples of the
coping mechanism we might call "change of place." In some individuals it can take the form of leaving the scene for long periods
of time in an attempt to get away from anxiety. Some people move
to other parts of the country, change colleges, take new jobs elsewhere, or travel extensively with this in mind. If the anxiety is very
threatening and if the sources of it are largely unconscious, change
of place can be an irrational, repetitive type of personality defense.
But in other circumstances and for other people it can be more
flexible and conscious. Joseph Kramer used it more in the latter
sense, and for him it had adaptive consequences because it
enabled him to keep his tension under control and continue his
effective study procedures.

Another way of relaxing was through dating. We noted that
Joseph had an active social life in high school, but he came to
Harvard unencumbered by a romance with a girl at home. He start-
ed dating regularly in his freshman year, by going to mixers at
Radcliffe and other women's colleges and using these contacts to
meet other girls. Movies or plays, dinner, and occasionally a lecture

were the main dating activities, and once Joseph got his car it was easier to go to places other than Radcliffe. In all of his Harvard career he dated only sparingly at Radcliffe, and the person who became his "steady" and eventually his wife attended one of the "Seven Sisters" colleges. It was not entirely clear to us why he did not date more at Radcliffe, but we suspect that in order to relax he felt the need to get farther away, both physically and emotionally.

During the fall of his sophomore year he dated a girl named Rebecca on an occasional basis, and as the year progressed he spent more time with her. She was dating other men, one of them with some serious intention; she and Joseph had trouble communicating, and by the end of sophomore year the romance nearly broke up. Rebecca wrote him during the following summer, however, suggesting that they talk things over in the fall, and slowly the romance grew in junior and senior years to an engagement for marriage. This sequence was not as simple as our brief account here might indicate, because the difficulties in the spring of sophomore year were associated with a depression on Joseph's part, but we shall return to that when we consider the occasions during which his adaptive mechanisms did not work effectively.

Joseph found different satisfactions in dating than did Jason Jellinec. Joseph was searching for companionship, for someone to take his mind off his work, and for sexual gratification. Jason looked more for emotional closeness, the chance to share feelings and to be accepted and understood. Joseph did not get close to many girls, if any, until he finally fell in love with Rebecca.

Although Joseph was not an athlete of varsity caliber, he enjoyed athletics and exercised regularly by playing squash or basketball. He liked the pleasure of physical activity as well as the competition and the fun involved in doing these things in company with others. Often he would read for awhile in the afternoon, then go to the Indoor Athletic Building for an hour or so, then study again before dinner. These things were fun for him as well as a way of relieving tension.

Our account thus far has stressed two dominant features of Joseph's life at Harvard and has focused on overt behavior and on conscious coping that he carried out. Before going further with his college experience, we might consider other information about his personality structure and speculate about the reasons for his behavior. The Rorschach and T.A.T. are helpful in that task.

In the freshman year, his response to the inkblots was guarded; he limited the number of responses he gave and was overprecise in the quality of his percepts. He seemed to have an uneasiness about commiting hemself to a percept that might be vulnerable to criticism. His emphasis was on the formal accuracy of responses to the blots and on a logical analysis of the things he saw. Dr. McArthur, the examiner, commented that this approach was a defense against interference by his impulses, which seemed to pose a threat to him. The nature of his response indicated that he felt threatened by aggression, which was associated with a conflict about dependency. As a consequence of his guarded or limiting style, his intellectual functioning was impaired to the extent that it was not as free for complex abstract thinking as that of many other students. But the Rorschach protocol also indicated that Joseph had some intellectual ambition, that he had good tactical intelligence, and that his perception of reality was basically sound.

The unwillingness for emotional commitment and further illustration about his conflict over dependency were to be found in many of his T.A.T. stories. As is so frequently the case, his story to Card 1 is a good illustration.

> Before I looked at the instrument I saw the child's face. I thought of a school child, typically a European, or more typically a French school child. The face didn't look like what we consider conventionally American. I saw *The 400 Blows* recently, about French schools, and I've read a lot about French schools, knowing that they're the toughest and all. Well, the violin and his expression seem to match. Well, I will assume that his father is a violinist, and has been playing, and left his violin on the table and gone out of the house. And the boy, who also has a love of playing the violin, sits down, admiring, not daring to touch his father's violin, and admiring it as if it were a Stradivarius or so. And, ah, by his expression, I don't think he will touch it as might be supposed.

As a working hypothesis, we might conclude from this story that Joseph saw much in his father to be admired and to be feared, but could not yet bring himself to compete actively with his father.

In other stories Joseph was hesitant about details, often posing two or three alternative plots and having difficulty in deciding which one to use. Also, most of his stories had ambiguous endings; or, if an ending contained a successful solution, it usually did not describe the means by which the outcome was achieved. Yet his stories also portrayed people who had energy available for constructive action, and the plots were organized around realistic themes. In reading the stories we had the impression of capacities that were being held back until certain issues were settled.

Both Rorschach and T.A.T. had some indications of free-floating anxiety. By and large, Joseph's emphasis on logicalness and accuracy and his wariness about commitment tended to keep the anxiety in check and prevent it from being disabling. We might anticipate, however, that environmental events could upset this balance and that, when it happened, symptom formation might occur. Dr. McArthur thought there were indications in the Rorschach of a vulnerability to somatic reactions.

This personality structure has features very much like those we associate with the obsessive-compulsive type. Certainly Joseph was far more compulsive than Jason Jellinec, but less so than would be typical in a patient population. We have noted also that his personality had many adaptive features for the Harvard environment. It will remain to be seen how much loosening might occur by time of graduation.

Joseph's study patterns are more readily understood in the light of the information from the projective tests. Identification and competition with his father provided motivation for his academic drive and were at the same time a source of anxiety because of the fear of his aggressive impulses. That anxiety could be kept in check by emphasizing rational control and scheduling and by ignoring or denying active involvement with his emotional life. Although the initial reason for his compulsiveness was control of anxiety, that behavior was also highly adaptive to some of the demands of the Harvard environment. Furthermore, Joseph had sufficient flexibility to recognize the need to keep his tension at reasonable levels by getting away from the area where his conflicts were strongest, that is, the academic environment.

This dynamic balance between anxiety and defenses is always sub-

ject to disequilibrium if something in the environment triggers an
increase in the anxiety or if the coping mechanisms are ineffective.
Just before Christmas vacation of his freshman year, Joseph had a
period of depression that lasted for several days, longer, he said, than
was usually the case. He felt that he was behind in his work to the
extent that he might do badly on his mid-year exams, badly at least
in relation to his high aspirations. For these few days his study pace
slowed, but he was then able to intensify his efforts again, and he
shifted his place of study from his room to the library. That worked,
and he did well on his exams.

In the fall of his sophomore year, he had a prolonged gastrointes-
tinal disorder for which he sought medical help. After a careful work-
up, his physician concluded that it was psychosomatic in nature and
that his symptoms would subside as the year went along. Joseph
said that at the time he did not feel particularly depressed or tense,
but during the spring of that year his depression returned, and it was
the most severe of any that he had during college. It continued inter-
mittently during the following summer and then almost disappeared
during his junior year.

An explanation of the cause of these depressive episodes is highly
speculative because Joseph never gave us easy access to his feelings.
At least two things may have been causative. First, he had found out
that he could do superior academic work at Harvard and this forced
him to think about the rest of his Harvard career and of the future.
To this extent, his depression was like the sophomore slump that
many students seem to have. In his case, the feeling of competition
with his father was probably heightened because he realized that he
could do as well academically as his father had done and therefore
would have to declare his independence in the near future. Coupled
with this could have been a sense of guilt that he had done so well,
perhaps even better than his father. Second, it was during this year
that he began to date Rebecca with some seriousness, only to find
that he was in competition with another man. That he might lose
this competition or that Rebecca might reject him was a serious
threat, even though he did not speak of her at that point in terms of
marriage. When Rebecca began to respond more affirmatively to
his advances during the summer and in the fall of his junior year,
much of this threat was removed.

The relationship with Rebecca proved to be an important factor in Joseph's ability to accept more fully the emotional side of his personality. He found in her a person who would accept him without his feeling any need to prove himself. Furthermore, she was a stable person and thus imparted a calming and strengthening influence when he felt upset. By the end of his junior year he described the situation as follows:

> She herself does not get deep depressions. Consciously or unconsciously she does a very good job of relaxing me. I suppose she allows me to run off whatever is irritating me, specific things, whatever they are. She'll listen and not object, even though some of the things may be highly exaggerated. So I can let off any excess energy.
>
> I think she knows me. I don't feel the same impetus to enforce my desires or opinions that I do in activity here. I feel I can talk to her without putting on any conventional pretensions. I can say whatever is in my mind—to present an unfinished thought—whatever comes to my mind. And nine times out of ten it's completed in her mind. At least I feel it is. I don't have to force her to be able to understand what I'm trying to say. At first it was a battle of wits on any discussion we had, but I don't feel it has to be that anymore.

Now to return to Joseph's Harvard experience. After his sophomore slump, he maintained a steady academic pace. Because he had a business career in mind, he thought that government would be an appropriate field of concentration. In addition, he took courses in economics and history and fulfilled his language and science requirements. His grades were good, all B's and A's, and he felt that it would be a good idea to write a senior honors thesis. His topic involved extensive library research, some of it in Washington, on a topic of trade treaties between the First and Second World wars, in contrast to the personal interviewing that was behind Jellinec's thesis. He gathered some of the data during the summer preceding his senior year and worked steadily at the project in the fall and winter. His tutor was helpful, but only as an adjunct, again in contrast to Jellinec, whose tutor had played a central role. Joseph told the interviewer in the fall that he wanted to get his thesis finished early in March so that he could go over the next-to-final draft with care before it was submitted, and indeed he did. The thesis was submitted two weeks early!

The meaning of the thesis to him and the high *magna* grade that he received on it had several facets. It proved to him beyond a doubt that he could match or surpass his father, with his advanced degrees from European universities. He was not entirely conscious of that fact, but it was at this time that he discussed quite openly with the interviewer his feelings of growing equality with his father. We have reason to suspect that the success of the thesis freed him to some extent from his fear of competition. He was not as aware of the emotional impact of this intellectual exercise as was Jason Jellinec, primarily because he was not as introspective and not as attuned to the emotional impact of events. Nonetheless, it was a crucial emotional event for him.

Throughout his four years at Harvard, he did not make any really close friends, other than Rebecca. He had good relationships with his roommates, had many acquaintances for bull sessions or for going to the movies, but none of these, he said, would be friends that he thought he would have much interest in after college. They were not as close as friends he had made in high school, many of whom he knew would remain close to him later in life when everyone had finished college and settled down into jobs and family life. The impression one might get from this is that friendships meant more to him if he thought they would be useful or would touch in some important way on his life. This did not mean that Joseph was cold and calculating or completely instrumental in his relations with people, but rather that his approach to things was in a rational, analytic way, not with an expressive or emotional response. He was not as concerned with people and interpersonal relationships as Jason was, yet he was an effective, generally happy, and likeable person.

Joseph's reaction to Harvard is an illustration of the manner in which the characteristics of a particular environment can affect the process of adaptation by a particular person. Early in the freshman year he told us that before he came he had heard Harvard was impersonal and he had not liked that idea, but that after a month at the College he liked the impersonality because of the freedom it gave him. This was a theme he reiterated throughout the four years. "They wouldn't miss you if you left for two weeks," he said, and added that he thought Harvard had the goal of forcing a student into situations where he had to rely on himself, to learn to think on his own without crutches of any sort.

A related theme he brought up a number of times was that Harvard did not offer easy ways for a student to become prominent. He was surprised to find out some of the important things his classmates had done. In general, such things were kept in the background. Furthermore, there was no particular activity that was the most prestigious, nor was there any organization known to be composed of student leaders. Also, there was no building or place around the Square that served as a central congregating place for students. Joseph did not say it, but this situation underlined the emphasis on freedom and individuality.

Joseph was quite accurate in his perceptions, from what we know about Harvard. That is not the point. He chose to make an issue of this, whereas Jason said little if anything about it in his interviews. Joseph's remarks reflected the struggle that he was having with becoming independent from authority. Also, the freedom gave him the opportunity to control his activities, to be as compulsive as he might wish, and to get away from Harvard whenever he wanted. A more constraining or directive environment would have limited these adaptive efforts.

Personality Change

The growth experience for Joseph Kramer was primarily a process of *consolidation* and *accretion* rather than reorganization or change. There were a few changes, which we will discuss shortly, but they were of relatively minor importance in terms of his overall personality structure. The knowledge he gained from his courses, from the social aspects of the Harvard environment, from the cultural events in Boston, and from the students and teachers with whom he came in contact helped him become "more of the same." He used Harvard primarily as a place to accumulate knowledge rather than to broaden his reference group and to effect social change as Jason had done.

As we have indicated, the structure of his personality was such that he was not very open to change; in fact, he resisted it. By not joining any social groups or organizations other than in name, by not being willing to become obligated to outside activities, he narrowed the range of possibility for change. His growth occurred in those areas where he had succeeded in the past and which worked effectively for him at Harvard.

Further indication of lack of change is the fact that he did not deviate from his plan to return to his home city. At no time did he really ever consider an alternative. In the same fashion, he never thought much about another occupation than his father's business. He mentioned law in his sophomore year, but we had the impression that he toyed with the idea in the spirit of trying out something different from his father's work. As his years at Harvard went by, the plan for returning to the family business settled more firmly and thought of the law receded.

The major psychological event for Joseph in his college years appeared to be the acceptance of his identification with his father. Certainly it was not complete by graduation, but much progress had been made. When he matriculated, he described the relationship with his father as one involving arguments about political issues. Joseph said that he tended to be on the conservative side, but not as much so as his father. Actually the differences between the two may have been exaggerated by Joseph's need, or perhaps the need on both sides, to get an argument going. During vacation periods the arguments would continue, but less was said about them by late junior and senior years. By then Joseph admitted that he and his father had abilities in common, even though he felt still that he was more like his mother in temperament. He did admit, however, that he thought he was becoming more like his father. Also, there seemed to be a greater acceptance by father and son of each other. With some satisfaction Joseph announced in his senior year that he had influenced his father to read some of the books that had appeared on his reading lists in courses in history and government.

Because of the importance of this identification in Joseph's growth, we might point to some of the prominent features of the elder Kramer. We have noted that he was an educated man. In addition to his technical training, he spoke a number of languages and was culturally sophisticated. He was well organized and a logical thinker, prudent in his business and yet imaginative enough to move continually ahead. Basically, he was a very stable person. He also had initiative and counteractive capacities. He had left Europe with little in the way of possessions, yet he was able to begin again in the United States and within twenty years to develop a flourishing manufacturing business. In the family ethos, the overcoming of adversity was an ever-present though little talked about theme. As noted at the beginning of the chapter, his father appeared to have little bitterness about the European tragedy. He did not let such feelings drag him down or impede his efforts in a new life.

Thus, Joseph had a strong figure with which to identify, strong not only in terms of activity and control, but also in terms of stability and integration. Sometimes such figures can be overwhelming to the developing adolescent. Joseph felt some of that pressure, but the positive features of the relationship were compelling and formed the core around which Joseph could eventually build his own identity.

Now a word about the changes in our student that he perceived and that we could document from our data. He looked back over the four years as follows:

> Well, of course I've seen something I never saw at home. I was intellectually motivated at home by grades, pretty much entirely. Up here I found that I gradually picked up the intellectual curiosity. I think I will hold onto it, to be curious enough to want to know something, at least a dilettante's knowledge of all the basic fields of inquiry. I certainly think my abilities here to write and express myself have picked up tremendously. Some sort of polish or sophistication I've picked up, at least in regard to the things I've studied. I've certainly met a different type of person. Socially, I don't know if I've changed all that much. I think I've become more aware of myself. I'm certainly more introspective than I was four years ago. Now I tend to see my own peculiarities. At times I've worried for a time that I was latently manic-depressive, particularly late in the sophomore year. But this year was easy.

His comments about introspection are interesting in the light of some data from the fall term of his sophomore year. At that time, the interviewer asked him how he felt about himself and if there had been any change since he came to Harvard. His immediate response was: "Oh, that's difficult. What do I think of myself? That's really hard to say. I don't—I can't think of anything immediately now."

That he had opened up some by senior year is indicated by the results on some of the "paper and pencil" tests. For example, between freshman and senior year he shifted from 26 to 39 on the psychological-mindedness scale, from below the class mean to somewhat above. At least we can say that he became more willing to endorse statements that emphasized interest in psychological processes.

A greater sensitivity to emotions and feelings as they influence behavior was reflected on shifts in scores from freshman to senior years on three sets of scales from the Myers Briggs Type Indicator. The first set comprises *sensation* and *intuition;* the former emphasizes knowledge gained through the five senses, the latter stresses conclusions derived by more unconscious processes. Joseph dropped from 19 to 13 on sensation and moved from 11 to 14 on intuition. *Thinking* and *feeling* represent the logical, analytical approach as opposed to the reliance on emotional nuances and sensitivity. His thinking score dropped from 17 to 12 and his feeling score rose from 3 to 10. On scales for *judging* and *perceiving,* the first deals with weighing, comparing, and sorting out, and the second with an emotional sensing of the qualities of a situation. Joseph shifted from 28 to 16 on judging and from 0 to 13 on perceiving. These data lend further support to the idea we have noted from the interview material, that some loosening of impulse life had occurred by graduation. He would probably never become a particularly flexible person, but he was considerably less rigid.

Two other changes should be mentioned. On the FIRO, Joseph went from 1 to 7 on *wanted control* and from 0 to 4 on *expressed control.* This kind of shift was characteristic of the class as a whole, as was a greater acceptance of emotionality and impulse expression. We have suggested that the overall findings indicate both a greater comfortableness with impulse life and a more acute sense of reality in the awareness of the need for control. That Joseph reflected the general trend is particularly interesting when we remember the themes from his freshman T.A.T., where anxiety about domination and the need for autonomy were prominent. The shifts on the control scales suggest that the dependence-autonomy issue was not so crucial for him by senior year, that he could see better the relationship between control by others and assertion of himself.

Concurrently, Joseph went from 1 to 5 on *wanted affection* on the FIRO. With less pressure from the dependence-autonomy issue, he was freer to accept the expression of love toward him by others. Certainly, the change in the score of this scale is not surprising in view of the growing affection between Rebecca and him, particularly from his junior year onward. By graduation he was much readier for accepting intimacy, in Erikson's terms.

In comparison with Joseph's self-assessment of change and the data from "paper and pencil" tests, we might look again at the projective material, the Rorschach and T.A.T. He increased quite markedly in the number of responses to the Rorschach. The psychologist commented that "now he was talking to us," in contrast to the "tight-lipped" approach he had used as a freshman. Thus, he was willing to be more revealing, although he continued his general approach of reluctance to go beyond what he viewed as the evidence. He was less accurate about the evidence, however, in his senior year. Dr. McArthur felt that there was much in the protocol to suggest that conflict and anxiety were now finding open expression. This anxiety limited his empathy, but at least he now was willing to let us know that he had conflicts about it. His control over this anxiety was far from perfect at the time of graduation, though his intellectualization was moderately effective.

The Rorschach responses suggested that the anxiety came from aggressive impulses, fear of harm, and black moods. Fear of the integrity of his body lay in the background. His compulsive personality style defended him against this anxiety; when given the right situation, one in which he could control things, he could function well. He found that situation at Harvard, and the shape of his life plans suggested that he would continue to do so.

The T.A.T. reflected this situation nicely. The stories to the first ten cards were quite conventional and much like those of his freshman year. The hero did not often take direct action for effective outcomes, which indicates the same unwillingness to commit oneself as in the beginning of Joseph's college career. The first half of the test thus reflected the working of his defensive structure. In the second half, where the stimulus pictures are much more ambiguous and suggestive of "wild" themes, the fear of aggression and bodily harm hinted at on the Rorschach came through, to a greater extent than in the freshman protocol. That it occurred only in the last part indicated that Joseph still kept it fairly well repressed, but that there was an increase over the freshman year suggested a greater willingness to face it, at least partially.

Comparison with Jason Jellinec

Throughout this case history we have made a number of comments about the differences between our first two subjects, but we have not made any systematic comparison with reference to our six variables of growth. Although the two men were different in many ways, they also had similarities.

By the time of graduation both had decided on marriage partners, but in other respects their *object relations* were qualitatively different. Jason was more outgoing, more involved, more intense in his dealings with others. His social involvement with peers and adults at Harvard was much greater; he used Harvard much as a surrogate extended family. Furthermore, Jason used identification to a much greater extent, both in numbers and in intensity of the identifications. Joseph mentioned no teachers or adults who were important to him while he was growing up and identified strongly only with his father, and then in a more guarded way. Each man changed little in the pattern of his object relations during college, and we would predict that their approaches to people would continue in the same manner.

Both men had positive feelings of *self-esteem,* although we did not find anything in Kramer that was comparable to the theme of the Homeric Hero. Joseph commented that in high school he imagined that other people thought and felt the way he did; thus he was not particularly self-critical. Also, he had experienced success and had numerous instances of competence in both academic and social areas. He knew when he was accepted by Harvard that it was on the basis of superior ability, and he anticipated no real difficulty in succeeding academically. We were left with a feeling, however, that Joseph's self-esteem was not as spontaneous as we had seen in Jason and was more vulnerable to the effect of defeat, disappointment, or ineffectiveness of his personality defenses. His self-esteem seemed to have more of a propped-up quality, as if effort was required to keep it high. Joseph, however, moved toward a stabilization of self-esteem as he came to his senior year because he

was able to handle his underlying anxieties better. Jason remained high throughout.

Neither man spoke of sharp *mood* swings prior to Harvard nor of
pronounced periods of depression. During college Joseph seemed
more subject to dark moods and for longer periods of time. Jason
had nothing comparable in length of time to the sophomore slump
Kramer experienced, which ran into the fall of his junior year. By
graduation, however, both men could be characterized as stable
in mood.

Our two men were quite different in *interest patterns,* and neither changed appreciably in these patterns. On the Strong Vocational
Interest Blank, Joseph had high scores on relatively few scales.
Those few were concerned with business detail, scales like banker,
C.P.A., and office manager. He had quite low scores in areas where
Jason was high, occupations concerned with various forms of social
service. He also had low scores, or "reject" patterns, as did Jason,
for occupations in professional areas or the sciences. Thus Joseph
did not have either the wide-ranging interests of Jason or his orientation toward people. For both men, their occupational choice fulfilled their pattern of interests.

As to *goal-directed behavior,* our two men had future goals in
mind when they entered college, although the substance of these was
not the same. Both were on the conservative side in value orientation, tending to emphasize the importance of work and of future
time orientation. Joseph saw college as an integral part of goal attainment, which included business school, a return to that part of
the country in which he had been reared, and a place in the business and social life of the community. In college one acquired the
necessary tools, frame of mind, and passport to later accomplishment. Jason also viewed college as preparation for the future, and
thus they both used college in an instrumental way in relation to
future goals. Jason, however, had a clearer idea of what he wished
to do by senior year than when he started, whereas Joseph was
fairly certain from the beginning.

Both men used obvious *control* mechanisms, but of different
kinds and with different intensity. Joseph Kramer rarely showed
anger and to our knowledge never lost his temper, whereas
Jellinec could get very angry at times and on one occasion was
thrown out of a game for contesting an umpire's decision and los-

ing his head while doing it. Both men accepted their sexual impulses and found expression for them, although Jason at one point in his junior year was in some conflict about this. Generally speaking, Kramer was more vulnerable to anxiety about impulses and worked harder to control them.

As for directing energy, both men knew what they wanted and how to get there, but Kramer was more narrowly oriented and considered fewer alternatives. He was less open to new possibilities from the environment and less able to use them if they occurred. Jellinec was more flexible in directing his energies.

The same theme continues in management of tension, for Kramer's defensive structure was more rigidly developed than was Jellinec's. It was very effective when environmental conditions were right, but he was not as capable of dealing with unexpected events.

In these three areas of control, neither man changed much during college. Both were somewhat more aware of their impulse life by graduation, but the basic ego strategies for handling feelings and directing energies continued much as they had in freshman year. They happened to be men whose character structure was well fixed.

When we move from the matter of control to a consideration of general adaptive style, Joseph tended to bring from the past a way of dealing with the world that did not change much. His way of adapting was to find a set of conditions where his logical, controlled approach would work. Going back to his home city and into his father's business was one way of fulfilling that. In doing so he could continue to plan in advance, know all the details, find controlled expression for his feelings, and work very much by himself.

Jason, of course, was more expressive, more willing to use feelings, and adapted through his interactions with people. He was more likely to seek new situations and to find people in these situations to help him and work with him. He was able to alter his background experience to fit new environmental demands and to effect in his life a rather striking social change. He fitted into an environment; Joseph had to find an environment that he could be happy in.

In describing the lives of different people and how they deal with the world, it is all too easy to make comparisons of healthier or less healthy, to judge one as better or more effective. It may be impossible entirely to eliminate such biases from case descriptions. We have tried to avoid it as much as possible, however, and to put the emphasis on variations in adaptive style within given environmental conditions. Neither Jason Jellinec nor Joseph Kramer is necessarily characteristic of Harvard students in general, but they do show how past experience can be utilized in adaptation and how different people can utilize present experience to fit their needs and ways of coping with the world.

Chapter 6 / George Parker

The remark often made by George Parker was that Harvard placed too much emphasis on the academic side of things and on grades. In his junior year he became quite annoyed with his tutor, who seemed not to understand why extracurricular activities might interfere with getting tutorial papers written. He thought the tutor was much too narrow and rigid. For Parker, there was a lot to learn about living that was not in books. Besides, college should be fun, the one remaining time when a person could be a free spirit. This was the time to kick up one's heels a bit. He intended to graduate from college, with a reasonable academic average if possible, but he would not be a grind. Some observers of higher education would characterize him as a "collegiate,"[1] a type less in evidence now than a decade or so ago.

George made a variety of impressions on the research staff. He joked with the secretaries and teased them while sitting with studied

1. Clark and Trow have defined four college subcultures: academic, vocational, nonconformist, and collegiate. The last is characterized by skill in interpersonal relations and the enjoyment of social activities, which are regarded as important for a career. Intellectual and vocational aspects of college are minimized. See Burton Clark and Martin Trow, "Determinants of College Student Subculture," Center for the Study of Higher Education, University of California at Berkeley (mimeographed). Also, the reader is referred to David Gottlieb and Benjamin Hodgkins, "College Student Subcultures," in Kaoru Yamamoto (ed.), *The College Student and His Culture* (Boston: Houghton Mifflin, 1968), pp. 238–255.

informality on the corner of one of their desks. The tempo of things picked up as soon as he appeared, for his coming was always an event, and there were emotional ripples in the office staff for a time after he had gone. He was not handsome, he even worried that he might be ugly, but people paid little attention to his looks. Some of the senior staff thought he was a bit arrogant, as though he were condescending to help out the research. Some called him brash and cocky and waited for him to get his comeuppance. Often a research subject seems to blend into the mass and is remembered years later with some difficulty. Not George Parker; no one forgot him.

The initial impression one gained from the interviews was that George's behavior was disorganized, that he pursued a great variety of activities, and that he jumped from one activity to another as the spirit moved him. His development did not appear to be as orderly as either Jellinec's or Kramer's, but it was much more fluid. In truth, he had the capacity for organization; in activities that he liked, he could be very successful, but this did not apply to the academic side of college. He used Harvard and the college experience in quite a different way from our first two cases, used it for a kind of social moratorium, with little worry about the effect of poor grades on a future career. In many ways his personality was more complex than either Jellinec's or Kramer's, and he had more of a problem in stabilizing his identity. In his own way, however, he had strong continuity with his past and an effective style of adaptation, even though his case history is in some contrast to our first two.

Home and School Background

George's boyhood was spent in a small city in eastern Pennsylvania, too far for commuting regularly to the metropolitan areas but where there were a few artists, writers, and retired urbanites. He went to public school there, of his own choice, for his parents gave him the option of boarding school if he wished. The high school was small and George was a leader. Though he never said so, we suspected that he did not want to lose the prestige and prerogatives that went with his position by going away to school. He indicated that these years in school were not without controversy. He had a penchant for expressing himself rather strongly on issues and for going ahead in situations without always checking with others in advance. Some teachers liked his liveliness. Others resented his interference and his brashness. From all indications, the school principal and George had something of an armed truce, although his transgressions were minor from a disciplinary point of view. In typical manner, however, George may have exaggerated things to the interviewer for dramatic effect.

His early high school years were academically uneventful. But in junior year, after his brother went away to college, George suddenly decided that he wanted to go to a good college and started giving some serious consideration to his studies. He still had time for dates and parties and working on cars, but he managed at graduation to win most of the prizes that "weren't specifically designated for girls." He ascribed this partly to the fact that his class was small and the work not too difficult, and he denied the fact that he was a grind. The evidence was clear, however, that when he wanted to do so he could work very effectively.

As George described them, the members of his family were rather colorful, at least in comparison to the Jellinec and Kramer families. There was a great deal of social activity in the house. The children felt comfortable about bringing friends home, and as they grew older, the Parker house became the place for parties large and small. People just naturally congregated there. House guests were always welcome, and vacations from college would always find at least one guest, if not more. Socially, the Parkers were relaxed and informal, always ready for a good time.

The children had always been given a good deal of freedom in their activities and in their choice of friends. On the other hand, they were not given everything they asked for or exempted from household responsibilities. As soon as they were able, in terms of size and age, they were expected to work after school, take summer jobs, and contribute from their own earnings to major personal purchases. Not long after he obtained his driver's license, George was bound and determined to have a car. His mother thought his choice was foolish and told him so, but let him go ahead anyway. He paid for it out of his own pocket, as well as for the subsequent numerous repairs and towing charges. Apparently his mother never countered with "I told you so," and George redoubled his money-making efforts and his knowledge about cars. As he reflected on these things in one of the interviews, he said that his father had always been willing to give him money for necessary things and paid his college expenses cheerfully, but that he expected to be repaid on loans that George asked for. He also made it clear that his son should run his own car and take care of such extraneous expenses. It is interesting that when some of his college friends were delinquent about repaying loans to him, George was quite indignant.

The elder Parker was a lawyer, a graduate of a first-rate Eastern school, and grudgingly accepted by his colleagues as an able and effective adversary. He had had offers to join good firms in the city but preferred the proximity of the country and the independence afforded him by his own practice. He was a gregarious person, well known in the community by people from all walks of life. No one could accuse him of being a snob. He worked hard at his law practice, but when the time came to relax, he could leave the legal problems behind while on the golf course or in a trout stream.

Mrs. Parker had been an accomplished pianist at one time but had put marriage and a family ahead of a career. She played little anymore because her standards were high and she could not satisfy them without constant practice. Her energy and artistic sensitivity found outlets in quite a different channel, the making of neckties. She was constantly on the lookout for unusual materials and had a workroom over the garage. Her label was much sought after in some of the specialty shops of New York and Philadelphia, but she had always resisted "going big time." She worked as the spirit moved her, more than just a hobby but short of a real business. She had a moderate independent income from her own family. George had a secret admiration for her work, though he thought that she was too impulsive and flighty to make a good businesswoman.

Two sisters and a brother rounded out the immediate family, although aunts and uncles and grandparents often visited. George did not feel that the family was particularly close-knit, not because of tension but because of the emphasis on independence. There had been some open sibling rivalry while the children were growing up and more than one fight. The parents were inclined to let these situations work out by themselves rather than to repress them. Nor did they take sides. George felt that he had to prove and defend himself, and when he was about ten he had a confrontation with Geoff, his older brother. George said that "he hit him a good one" and that after that he left him alone. We have some reason to suspect, however, that the rivalry continued on a more subdued level. He commented later, "I never did anything till I got rid of him."

The Parker family was very much a part of the community. According to the standards of the city, they were somewhat unconventional, but secretly envied rather than discriminated against. They combined their freedom and openness with a sense of civic responsibility and a capacity for hard work. Both parents not only worked on the standard charity drives but also served on special commissions for the schools, and Mr. Parker was a member of the mayor's advisory council on zoning and industrial expansion. Most people in town knew the Parkers well enough to call them by their first names. They were solidly entrenched in the city and planned to stay. George never indicated that his parents' position gave him any special privileges, nor did it particularly put him on the spot. His differences of opinion with the school principal he recognized as the result of his personal style, not as a reaction to family social status.

The Parkers had always more or less assumed that their offspring would go to college. George gave it little thought until the summer after his sophomore year in high school, when he realized he would have to make a mark if he was to be admitted to the college of his choice. He felt pressure, in a subtle way, but never indicated that he felt it oppressive or inappropriate.

George had a good all-around record as he came to Harvard. In addition to scholastic honors, he had entered and won the state science fair. Not only did he work on cars but he also used his mechanical skills and energy in his senior year in high school to start a modest contracting business in his hometown for small repairs and building jobs. He also was a lifeguard and taught swimming. As we noted, he had time for dating, although he was inclined to play the field and did not have a steady girl when he matriculated.

The Harvard Years

George came into a familiar environment because his older brother, Geoffrey, had already preceded him at Harvard. He also had some definite ideas about his college experience: to take four years and "shop around" as much as possible, not to study too much, and to involve himself in a number of extracurricular activities. Eventually, he thought he might go into business, or follow his father into law, and then perhaps try to make a career in politics.

True to his word, he did not study much in his freshman year and seemed delighted to tell the interviewer how far behind he was on reading assignments or what poor grades he received on papers or hour exams. Accompanying this recital, however, were hints that he had some conflicts about the results of academic work. He noted a number of times that there was no parental pressure to get good grades, and we felt that he was making more of this than the case warranted. He also said that he thought he might make dean's list sometime before he graduated, but that if he achieved that goal, he would never tell anyone. Like Jason Jellinec, George managed not to flunk any courses, but his academic average the first year was very low.

In place of studying, George did a number of other things. One of them was sleeping. He claimed that he was tired after a strenuous summer and that he had a lot of catching up to do. Indeed, he always seemed tired, and his interviews were punctuated regularly by yawns. The latter behavior was a characteristic that persisted through much of his four years with us and caused us to speculate that the need for sleep may have had a defensive quality about it, as a protection against getting too involved or letting his feelings about people become too obvious. In retrospect, we also remembered that he was now back in open competition with Geoff but not yet in a position to confront him and beat him again.

Otherwise, he spent a lot of time having fun and doing things on the spur of the moment. Friends were always dropping in from Pennsylvania, or there was a beer and bull session, or he had to do some work on the car he and his brother shared. In the winter there were ski trips to New Hampshire and Vermont. At times he drank rather heavily, and he often courted injury by driving too fast or being reckless in skiing. There seemed little organization or rationality to all this, and George recounted it in a jocular manner, with many laughs (as well as yawns). He was an able raconteur. And, we might add, his way of life was at the opposite end of the continuum from Joseph Kramer.

George was also quite bitter about one of his roommates; at one point in the year thay had a fight, with words only, but it sounded as though Parker was rather angry. Neither Jellinec nor Kramer had ever come to such open conflict. George was annoyed because he felt the man was a social climber who tried to impress others with his background and his connections. This was a theme that appeared quite often in the four years—that is, George's inveighing against social snobs and asserting that social position did not mean much to him. It was hard to judge to what extent the room-mate was overbearing and how much George was reading into the situation some of his own conflicts. At least the fight cleared the air enough for workable relations in the roommate group, if not for close ones.

One final note about the first year. George commented in the spring interview that he aspired to some positions of leadership and responsibility, like the ones he had held in the past, which he had lacked during his first year. He certainly had the aptitude and experience for such behavior, even though he had studiously avoided it as a freshman.

When the second year was over, Parker looked back and con-cluded that it had been an unhappy year as it balanced out, not all bad but without the fun of the first year. He continued his lacka-daisical approach to course work, being constantly behind. He said that he too often gambled that he could get the work done on time and sometimes got caught short on hour exams. He had chosen history as a field of concentration and had four reading courses, plus a tutorial session that required extensive reading and papers. He spent many hours working on his car, and then, when he would sit down to read, he often fell asleep. Even so, he managed to pass and actually may have done more work than he liked to admit to us.

He quit the tutorial in November because there was considerable work to do, he was not getting credit for it, and he did not particu-larly like the tutor. He said that he had "quite a row" with his tutor but in reality the tutor did not seem to be that disturbed, as George later admitted. We sensed that he had a need to dramatize the con-flict in the situation in order to underscore his own assertiveness and independence. He did have a bit of a chip on his shoulder for authority figures. At any rate, with the dropping of the tutorial he effectively ruled himself out of the honors program and the possibility of writing a senior thesis. He said that anyway he did not want to write a thesis on a confined topic; instead, "while I'm here I'd rather meet as many people, and see as many things as I can, and not spend a lot of time just sitting around on one individual topic."

During this year his brother dropped out of Harvard, an incident about which George had quite mixed feelings. On the one hand, he was angry at Geoff because he had let his father down, had not taken some of his exams, had not studied at all, and thus had wasted his father's money. Geoff had not kept up his responsibility on the car, so that George did almost all the work on it, with only half the usage. Yet he also seemed to have a sense of satisfaction in doing better than his brother and having his father tell him that he could work better than Geoff. This was not another confrontation, as when he was ten, but it had the same effect; George came off best.

Also, during this sophomore year a close friendship developed with one of his roommates, Todd Jackson, that was destined to continue through college—"closer than a close friend," as George said. They had many interests in common and shared some personal tragedy in Todd's family that elicited an empathic side to Parker not often visible. Todd was not a threat, academically or socially, and with him George could lower some of his barriers. We never could be sure how open he was in the friendship, because we never observed the two of them together, but George's interview accounts were regular in affirming the relationship without seeming to overstate the case.

One of the important events of his Harvard career began sophomore year; he found an outlet for his organizational abilities in a business venture. The Harvard Student Agencies is an office sponsored by the College that acts as a kind of holding company for a variety of student-run activities. The more commonly known ones are the bartending and catering services, charter flights at vacation times, and the publication of a guide to traveling in Europe, a knowledgeable and lively book based on student experience. Students run the various agencies for profit; the better run, the greater the profit, given a good market. This was a natural for George Parker, and he started working with the bartenders group, which at the time was not well organized. There was good pay, and good tips, in bartending, but even more could be made in managing the operation. That was his ultimate goal.

The interviews for these two years, and indeed for all of his Harvard career, contained constant references to his family. He claimed that the members were not close, but they certainly were in constant touch through visits and phone calls. He noted their activities, their reactions to events, and delighted in the annual family trip to a ranch in Wyoming. He spoke in admiration of his father and about their common interests, yet said they did not talk deeply about things. He cited a series of differences between himself and his sister Sue, just ten months younger, yet seemed to be very protective of her. He was somewhat disparaging of his mother's fussing over them all and not being able to control any of them, yet grateful for her concern. He complained and criticized, yet did not let go of the family, as though he wanted to be his own man but still found things in the family life that were important to him.

This pattern of life which we have been describing continued through junior and senior years. He gained the manager's job for the bartending group and spent a good deal of time reorganizing the advertising and the training program for new bartenders. Once that was accomplished, he was able to make nearly a thousand dollars a year from the enterprise, half again as much as the previous manager. Even with reorganization, the job still took about fifteen hours a week and was often on his mind. At least, he talked a lot about it in the interviews.

He also got involved in other extracurricular activities: in one of the political clubs, with WHRB, the Harvard radio station, and in the Hasty Pudding Club. In each case he worked hard when it was necessary and appropriate, but also found much time for joking and having fun. He was well regarded by his peers, not only for his sense of humor, but also for his organizational ability, and was elected to a number of responsible jobs. These activities, along with the bartending business, took a good deal of time but apparently brought equal satisfaction; as George remarked in his junior year, "Now things that take up my time are constructive, things that have a definite purpose." His somewhat plaintive remark in freshman year that he missed administrative responsibilities and his subsequent behavior indicated that he liked such activities and was becoming assured that he could do them in the adult world as well as he had done them in high school. He often remarked that he did better at some things than at others, especially at things that interested him. Most often such activities were logical, practical, everyday things that involved planning, organizing, and directing others. In many ways, his cognitive style was similar to Joseph Kramer's, although Kramer let it dominate his life, whereas Parker let it alternate with periods of apparent disorganization, at least with periods when he was more willing to be pushed by some of his impulses than by orderly control.

As George moved into his senior year and made a choice about a future occupation, many of the reasons he cited for law were, interestingly enough, like the satisfactions he had found in his extracurricular activities.

> Law is something that has evolved for years, centuries, and it is a direct reflection of life and of human relations. And it's not a theoretical reflection; it's a very interesting exercise, and a continuous exercise in logic. And I really enjoyed the law aptitude exam, where we had to decide which principles applied where, and so on. And it has a feeling of being mechanical in a way. I'm certain there are a good number of courses in law school that are very dull and just exactly what I'm taking in college, but there are also a certain number that—you know I used to enjoy debating and organizing facts—where there's a purpose, and the purpose is sensible and immediate.

He did not view his college courses as directly relevant to the study of the law, and indeed felt that many of them were quite irrelevant, too abstract and theoretical. Thus, he was not motivated to study hard, because he was not really interested and did not feel that it was worth grinding away at his studies just to get accepted at a first-rate law school. He thought that in the long run his success in the law would depend more on his ability than on the place where he obtained his law degree.

The reader will remember that his father was a lawyer and a graduate of one of the leading law schools. It would be easy to assume that George's choice of the same occupation reflected his identification with his father, even as Joseph Kramer's choice of the family business was a result of identification. That conclusion, for both men, is too simple. Identification undoubtedly was involved, but their career choices also reflected a realistic utilization of abilities and of preferred cognitive styles. At the same time, the choices provided an opportunity for competition between father and son, although both students had some conflict about that competition. Parker's lack of concern about attending a prestigious law school may have indicated that he was uneasy about that conflict and had not resolved it by graduation. Kramer, by his senior year, seemed more comfortable with the fact that he would eventually take control of the business from his father.

Another theme, which we noted earlier, continued through Parker's four years: the tendency to pick fights with various people, a roommate or one of his instructors. The actions of others often annoyed him. In particular, he had difficulty in his junior year with his tutor, from whom he needed approval for his schedule of courses and from whom he took a non-honors tutorial. On three different occasions, George asked for the tutorial assignment, because he planned to attend the seminar: "Each time some problem with the agency I'm running came up, or something, and I was unable to attend, or unable to get the reading done, and he got, I think, justifiably annoyed. But on the other hand, it was something that wasn't required of me and I think he could have been a little more tolerant." George tried to evade some other requirements and got angry because his tutor implied that he really was not interested in working and was trying to find excuses to avoid studying. George felt that his social activities were an important part of college. He then commented that the tutor and many of his other instructors had not worked very hard to arouse his interest and that this was one of the failings of the Harvard teaching system. In the recounting of this incident, George seemed to be saying two things: leave me alone and let me do things my way, or make a special effort to inspire me.

He also continued fighting with one of his roommates, the same man as before, becoming annoyed with his sloppiness around the room, his slowness in paying his share of the phone bill or repaying loans that George had made to him, his social snobbery, and his criticism of George and the other roommates for the kind of life they led. We felt that George took a certain pleasure in "bitching" about such matters and sometimes used the situation as a way of attacking qualities in others that he was conflicted about in himself. To that extent, he needed a scapegoat. Underneath, he was uneasy about his disorganization, insecure about his social position, and anxious to prove his intellectual ability, but as yet he could not grapple openly with any of these issues.

One final aspect of his undergraduate years is important in our description of his life history—his dating relationships and his relations with women in general. Three women enter this theme: his mother, whom we have already characterized, his younger sister, and the girl he dated on a more or less steady basis. To take the last first, George maintained a relationship with Amy, a girl he had met at home who now attended a college in Connecticut. At times he spoke of the possibility of marrying her, but his words never seemed to carry very serious intent. He found in her a lively companion who was willing to do things on the spur of the moment, who liked to go to parties, and who found pleasure in her sexual impulses. She did not pressure George to change his ways or try to maneuver him into marriage; at least he never indicated to us that he thought she was trying to do so. Their relationship was not especially intellectual in nature, though George said that she was not dull. He gave us the impression that he was not yet ready to settle down and consequently kept the relationship with women he dated on the light side. He dated a number of girls from time to time, but always took Amy to the big parties and dated her on vacations at home; still, marriage was not yet for him.

His sister, Sue, had skipped a year of school in the early grades and consequently was in the same academic grade as George. They had been very close while growing up, and George obviously had a good deal of affection for her. It was interesting to observe, therefore, how George was constantly trying to differentiate himself from her; she was a good student, she was organized and less impulsive, she was more serious and had higher moral standards than he did, she was more naive about the ways of the world. He was quite concerned about the men she dated, assessing their qualifications for marriage and their character with a careful eye. Again, we felt that he made a great attempt to see her as more different from him than she actually was, as though the solidifying of his identify demanded it.

To some extent the same was true of his relations with his

mother; he did not talk about similarities in interests or temperament, as he did when speaking of his father. The subtle implication
of his remarks was that her control of the family was not very effective, and it was control that was a central issue in his development.
His disparagement of her seemed almost a way of projecting his own
uneasiness about control onto her. This went on through most of
his four years at Harvard, slowly changing at the end as he looked
more toward his own future and less toward the past.

By the time of graduation, George had firmly decided to go to
law school as soon as he finished his military service. The latter
was a point on which he and his father agreed, that it was part of
his citizenship and should be fulfilled. We must remember that the
sentiment against the Vietnam war had not in 1964 reached the intensity it later did, and we do not know how George would have reacted under the social pressures of today. His academic record was
only mediocre, and he was turned down in his long-shot application to one of the Ivy League law schools; thus he decided to wait
and make further applications when he had done his military
service.

As he thought back over the four years, he felt that change in
his personality had been only moderate. He said he had gained some
academic tools: a section man in sophomore year had taught him
how to write, and he had learned "how to analyze a piece of something." He had a more sophisticated approach to "life and things"
and had put some polish on his provincial Pennsylvania background.
He was not as reckless as he used to be, was somewhat more tolerant, and was probably better organized. This is not a striking cata-
logue of changes, but we saw some others that may have been out
of his awareness, and will now turn to an evaluation of his personality and the manner in which he handled certain developmental
issues.

Psychodynamic Issues

George Parker used Harvard in a rather old-fashioned way, at
least in a way that was more likely to have been used a decade or so
ago. For him it was a *socially provided moratorium* that allowed
for a good deal of fluidity and disorganization in his activities without undue academic pressure. This pattern had been frequent in

the age of the "gentleman's C," and in those days students with
the right kind of secondary school and family background could go
to Ivy League graduate schools on the basis of mediocre college
grades. Many have done so through the years and later become outstanding physicians, lawyers, and businessmen. But in 1964 the
pattern was becoming anachronistic, as indicated in part by Parker's
inability to get into a leading law school. The moratorium was still
important for him, however, because it gave him the chance to work
on certain underlying personality issues. He could still afford it,
financially and psychodynamically.

Parenthetically, it should be noted that George came by the
"collegiate" pattern quite naturally; it was like much of the life
style of his family. They were a bit unconventional and also a bit
upper-class, with an Eastern background and Establishment connections, people who were building a bit of New York in their corner
of Pennsylvania. They regarded college as the time for spirit and
for social activities as well as other pursuits, and they always seemed
to understand and accept George's escapades.

To a greater extent than our first two cases, George Parker had the
problem of establishing his identity. He did not go through a crisis
and did not risk identity diffusion, but he did have some underlying
differentiation and clarification to make. This took a number of
forms, one of the most important being an attempt to differentiate
himself from his father. This process was difficult for George because he and his father were very much alike in attitudes, behavior,
and outlook on life and would be alike in terms of career. In spite
of his father's unconventional style of life, he was basically a fairly
conservative man, and the son had the task of accepting the conserva-
tism and fitting it with his own value system. Here we see something
in common between Parker and Kramer; both had fathers who were
strong characters. Both viewed their fathers in a competitive sense,
but Parker's situation was complicated by the fact that he also
liked his father very much. Kramer never said, "My father is a hell
of a nice guy," as did Parker. Consequently, George found it more
difficult to confront the competition issue and become an autonomous person. By not studying hard at Harvard, he was able to delay an active competition with his father on the level of "work"
until he could sort through his feelings and decide how much he was
willing to be like his father.

A second theme was the necessity for separation from the feminine side of his background. Here we are dealing with two levels, for the projective tests indicated some kind of fairly deep-seated and unconscious fear of women and of destructiveness associated with mother figures. Possibly he was afraid of feminine aggressiveness, as Dr. McArthur felt was the case on the basis of his freshman Rorschach responses. The T.A.T. supports that hypothesis, and his story to Card 1 is a good illustration.

> Well, I suppose that the child's mother was teaching him to play the violin and that the cake was burning in the stove, so she locked him in his room, and he has fallen asleep over it.
>
> (E: What might have come out of this?)
>
> Oh, well he is going to get a whale of a lecture when she comes in, she might even burn the violin. She is the excitable type.

On a level somewhat closer to consciousness, we must remember his sister, with whom he was so close in age and schooling and who perhaps reminded him all too strongly of the feminine side of his nature. If we regard the problem simply as one of establishing a sexual identity, he had the task of working out an acceptable masculine role for himself. Thus his efforts to see himself as being as different as possible from his sister could be viewed in the service of that task.

George also needed to get free from his older brother, from the feeling he remembered during boyhood of being pushed around and dominated, and from the unease associated with the aggression that was aroused. Getting free had been a task that spanned years and began with his standing his ground when he was ten and "belting" his brother. It probably ended when Geoffrey could not do as well at Harvard and George quite definitely came out on top.

Finally, we noted that he had some anxiety about rejection and seemed unduly sensitive to the idea of an inferior social status. We were not sure of the source of this fear, whether it had something to do with his body image, the "little fat one," as he put it, or grew from his fear of feminity or from competition with his brother. Also, there were some indications that he felt his father's forebears were not of completely acceptable social status. At any rate, part of his identity resolution required the development of a self-esteem based on acceptance by his peers from all walks of life.

George thus had conflicts that came not only from fear of rejection, but also from fear of domination by women, from unease about intimacy, from fear of being beaten in competition as well as of losing control of his anger. These are not unusual fears in an adolescent or young adult, and they did not make Parker neurotic. They did, however, affect the manner in which he dealt with the world and the mechanisms he used for adaptation.

One way of protecting himself was to go into a shell, or at least to put up certain barriers that made it more difficult for other people to reach the real George Parker. The teasing and wisecracks served that purpose because they kept him from being serious and being committed. He often took the role of the critic, finding fault with Harvard or with his roommate, and that was another way of keeping distance. His need for sleep when he felt threatened was also a way of going into a shell, although we might infer from the T.A.T. story just quoted that he was not easy about that particular defense, because sleep was followed by punishment. We have already mentioned a further technique, that of projection—toward his mother, his roommate, and his tutor. Often, by picking fights, he could provide a target for his scorn and perhaps for things he did not like about himself.

On a more general level, his social life, his partying and lack of studying, his drinking and his dating, all kept him from becoming committed to the major reason for being at college, that is, the academic. These activities protected him as well by giving him time to work on developmental issues.

Had these been all the ego strategies that Parker had available, we might have anticipated the development of symptoms when the going got rough. He had excellent ability to plan and organize in matters that interested him, however. He was shrewd and practical and down to earth. He could work very hard when he wanted to. He used these qualities in his extracurricular activities and gained some real satisfactions for work well done and money made, as well as acceptance by his peers. To this extent, he does not fit the traditional "collegiate" pattern, because there were areas where he worked hard and accomplished much. We might also note that his attitude toward school work freed him from excessive scholasticism, the pattern into which Kramer fell, and thereby gave him more freedom for developing interpersonal relations.

The character of the environment sanctioned the adaptive process that George carried out. The "gentleman's C" tradition was still sufficiently alive to give a certain social legitimacy to his actions and thus partially to excuse them in the eyes of his instructors. Coupled with this was the emphasis on freedom, so that he could do as he pleased without anyone checking up on him, could cut all the classes he wanted while he slept or went on trips. He was called to account only for papers or examinations. Harvard is not unique among colleges in these attributes, although it may give more freedom from such academic requirements as class attendance than many colleges do. George had a rather ideal environment in which to carry out a social moratorium.

Personality Changes and Comparison with Other Cases

In common with our first two cases, George Parker had good *object relations,* although with variations. He did not have as much empathy as Jellinec and at the time of graduation was not yet ready for the intimate emotional relationship of marriage. He was, however, less afraid of women by then. Like Kramer, he came to identify with his father but with no adults at Harvard. Also, he was distinguished from the other two cases by the close friendship with a peer in college. The changes in his identity situation, vis-a-vis his father, brother, and women, indicated that his relationships with others in the future might become closer and less guarded.

Each of our first three cases had his own style. Parker was the extrovert, kidder, hail-fellow-well-met; Jellinec was sincere, straightforward, and enthusiastic; Kramer was introverted, cautious, logical, and compulsive. Each style served its user well, and it is impossible to say that one personality pattern was better than the others. Ways of dealing with the world must be judged in terms of a person's total life style.

George's *self-esteem* was high. He had done well in both studies and extracurricular activities in high school and knew that if he applied himself to a task he could accomplish it. He did not fear flunking out of Harvard as did Jellinec, but neither did he have athletic competence to fall back on. He was aware of interpersonal competence, knowing that he could successfully direct people. He did have some unease about being accepted socially, but it was a minor theme and by the end of college seems to have largely disappeared. Like Jellinec and Kramer, Parker had no major assaults on his self-esteem at Harvard, and he graduated with high spirits despite his mediocre grades.

We never saw George depressed, nor did he speak of having depressed periods like Kramer or Jellinec. It is quite possible that his ability to mobilize his anger in blaming others kept him from the guilt that often accompanies depression; that is, by making other people into "fall guys" for his shortcomings, he could alleviate some of his anxiety and tenseness. Neither of our first two cases used that approach. We could not say, on the other hand, that his *mood* was always pleasant, because at times his criticism could be biting and cynical. Nonetheless, in general his disposition was agreeable. His mood, furthermore, appeared to be quite stable, and when it did shift, it was in response to environmental factors more than to inner stimuli. Changes in mood over the four years were not as noticeable in Parker as in Kramer or Jellinec.

His pattern of *interests* on the Strong Vocational Interest Blank had some similarity to that of Jellinec; he scored high on scales in the social service group. He was also high on business detail, however, whereas Jellinec was not. By senior year, his score on the lawyer scale had also become high, but otherwise the pattern was essentially unchanged. Both men showed a greater range of interests than did Kramer.

For Parker, the effect of four years at college was to focus his interests within the general area of working with people. Being a lawyer would provide an outlet for that, in addition to satisfying his bent for practical and down-to-earth matters. If he eventually went into politics, the result would be the same. The focusing did not come about through courses or contact with teachers, but through his use of the moratorium to accept and integrate his identification with his father.

Our men were similar in keeping to *goals* about occupation and life style as they went through college, although Kramer was most definite about where and how he wanted to live. Parker talked about living somewhere in the East, probably Pennsylvania, but not in a large city, because he wanted easy access to the country. He saw himself entering into the social life of the community, much as his family did now, but he did not talk much about life with children, as did Jellinec.

In spite of apparent disorganization and fluidity, George had definite goals, and this fact may have been crucial in enabling him to use the social moratorium in a productive sense. He justified his low grades with the belief that his eventual success in law would depend less on the law school he attended than on his personal skill. He did not let the low grades deter him from his goal.

We might note here that all three men were very much future-oriented, even though Parker at times appeared to live only for the present. This fact was important in their ability to adapt, but we cannot necessarily draw the conclusion that such future-oriented goals are necessary to successful personality development. Many college students today emphasize the present, emphasize a being rather doing orientation, and through the goals derived from these values are able to adapt successfully. Assessment of the effect of goal-directed behavior on development must consider the particular life circumstances of the individual being studied and the climate of the environment at that time.

Parker was freer in impulse expression than our first two cases, when we consider his drinking behavior, his willingness to do things on the spur of the moment, his failure to meet many of his obligations, his willingness to pick a fight, and his sexual expressiveness. He was not impulse-ridden, however, and he did have adequate *control mechanisms.* For a time during the moratorium, he did not exercise these controls as tightly as he would later in life. Neither Jellinec nor Kramer could let themselves go in this way and perhaps did not need to.

On control through the directing of energy, we have behavioral data to indicate that George could do so effectively when he wished, and from the senior T.A.T. we have an indication that he will do so in his future. The story to Card 18 BM is a prototype of an organizing theme that appeared in a number of his senior stories. The picture shows a man being grabbed on the shoulders from behind by a number of hands.

> Tennessee Williams always has a character who has always been pushed around and eventually does become a very mean person fighting back . . . not necessarily mean, but . . . so let's say that what leads up to this is some kind of assumed background which means that this person is not socially elite, or he's, you know, doesn't have any money, and is always sort of being

pushed around, and he takes it for quite a while, and then something happens and he gets the taste of money. Perhaps it's from
some kind of legal activity, or from just some unusual circum-
stance. He gets the taste of power, and after this he will strive
to gain, make his way . . . and then of course he'll have to be
moral about it. So he'll either be unfair and very brutal and
animalistic in his attempts to make his way, in which case jus-
tice must prevail and he will fall into the den of iniquity . . .
or he will do it in a moral way, succeed and be a big business
man, big success story. Probably the theme of success is the
best one to extrapolate.

We have made a number of references to the techniques by which
Parker handled tension, and at the risk of some repetition we will
summarize them here. He kept himself somewhat aloof and unin-
volved in an intimate sense by being a critic and a joker, although
with a very close friend he could drop this shell. He appeared un-
serious and disorganized, which was one way to keep people off
while he pursued the task of working out his identity. In being the
critic, he could also use projection and blame the environment for
things that went wrong, thereby taking the heat off his own conflicts. This kind of management of tension limited his empathy and
left to the future his capacity to establish an emotionally intimate
relationship with a woman. At the same time, these traits could be
useful to him in the practice of law and may give us a preview of
the manner in which he would defend a client.

There were few changes in Parker's "paper and pencil" tests,
and he could not document many himself; still, we had the clinical
impression that some important things had happened to him at
Harvard, whose effects would be visible later. These changes might
be considered small at the moment, yet in the long-term span of
adaptation they were important. Dr. McArthur commented, in comparing his freshman and senior Rorschach protocols, that the same
conflicts were there, but by senior year they were better handled
and his character structure was more firm, "which will enable him
to use a kind of one-upmanship as a social and intellectual means
of coping." His ability to adapt was thereby strengthened.

We opened this case presentation by referring to George Parker's comment that there was more to college than grades. In retrospect, he was indeed right. Kramer could not have lived the way Parker did, nor could Jellinec. They had other business at college; the one to acquire tools for a later career, the other to find a home. Parker found a moratorium that helped him grow up.

Chapter 7 / Jonathan Thackery

One day in early May, when he was a senior at Harvard, Jonathan Thackery thought back over his four years at the college and reported to the interviewer a series of mixed reactions. He had enjoyed the freedom to write and the exciting tutorials. He had enjoyed taking part in the theater, in attending plays, and in producing and directing them. Some of his teachers had made a profound impression on him, particularly the man who guided his freshman seminar. It was fun to meet famous people at cocktail parties at the House functions. He was glad to have had the chance to write papers, stories, and plays. The trips away from Harvard had been exciting and were prominent in his memory: going skiing, going to the Cape or to New York, and even some longer trips to other parts of the country.

He said he would always come back, given the chance, to live these four years over again. He would always remember them, however, as being necessarily unpleasant much of the time because he could not feel at home with people at Harvard that he met through ordinary channels. He thought most people were too self-conscious, "too paranoid" almost. He could not make certain kinds of jokes without people feeling put off, and consequently he rarely said anything seriously except "in these depressing conversations" (the research interviews) or in hour examinations or analagous situations. He thought most people were on their guard, anxious not to have others make fools of them and anxious to impress

143

others with their erudition. He had been guarded as well and said that a close friend at home had told him before matriculation: "You know, they'll never catch on to you up there." He had replied that such a remark was "very flattering to his singularity," but he was sure he would adjust or they would understand. She had countered: "It's taken us twelve years." And he added that "she turned out to be right."

He concluded that on a day-to-day basis the Harvard environment had been boring, was too self-conscious, and lacked a sense of playfulness, but nonetheless had provided some of the most exciting moments of his life. The freedom was wonderful, even if it had led to wasteful years in terms of worthwhile activity; it was the freedom that he would always remember.

When we pondered the material in the interviews and psychological tests, we were impressed by the contrast in his personality development with our first three cases. Jonathan Thackery left Harvard having made relatively little progress in working through the tasks of adolescence, especially in establishing his identity in regard to work and sex roles. His development appeared to have been delayed, and when he graduated, we could not be certain whether this was a temporary pause or a more permanent limitation in character structure. Our indecision rested on very definite signs of creativity and strength in his personality and on real inhibitions in his capacity to relate to others and to structure life goals. We present his case in this book because he illustrates a type of developmental problem we saw in some other students and because he also shows the amount of fluidity and unpredictability that can appear at this point in the life cycle.

The Early Years

Jonathan was born and reared in Virginia, in a small city where the style of life and interpersonal relationships were Southern in orientation, but where there was also some moderation of the social attitudes characteristic of the Deep South at the time. On the paternal side of his family, there were a number of people who could be called eccentrics and some who had clinical psychopathology. There was alcoholism, marital instability, depression, and possibly some schizophrenia.

His paternal grandfather spent the last two decades of his life in

a mental hospital, his illness attributed to having been gassed in
World War I. The paternal grandmother committed suicide. His father, drafted into the army in World War II, had a "nervous breakdown" after being discharged and was hospitalized briefly. The most
general picture of the paternal relatives was of personality instability, which Jonathan recounted half with embarrassment, half with
relish, but also in a surprisingly candid manner. He had relatively
little contact with this side of the family, however, and most of his
information came to him at second or third hand.

He remembered his maternal grandparents as warm, comfortable
people, with whom he spent a number of summers at their place
outside the city. His grandfather had a way with animals and raised
purebred collies. He and Jonathan had long walks and talks, and
his grandfather "explained things" to him about the world of nature.
Both grandparents read to him from Golden books, took him to
church, and talked with him about local events.

Jonathan's father was an "engineer" with the public works depart-
ment of the city, having combined some correspondence courses
and practical experience to give him the necessary background for
that work. He was a quiet man, even passive in nature, except "when
he gets mad he just loses control of himself completely every two
months or so." Jonathan spoke little of him in the interviews, apparently not because he disliked him, but because he felt they had
little in common. His mother was more active socially, especially in
church affairs, but her life too was limited to the daily events of
home, church, and neighborhood. Jonathan indicated that he found
security and love at home, but also that he felt an intellectual gulf
he was never able to bridge. He knew they were proud to have him
enrolled at Harvard but also realized they had little or no concep-
tion of what his life was like in Cambridge.

When Jonathan was four, a sister was born, and another when he
was five. His memories of this period reflected some sense of boredom and loss relieved only by visiting his grandparents. But when
Jonathan was six, his grandmother died of cancer. The rediscovery
and reading of books appeared to be a source of comfort at this
period.

As Jonathan recounted his childhood and adolescence, the center
of activity appeared to be in the community and school. He remembered specific teachers with great clarity and spoke of the special
plays, pageants, and concerts they performed in the primary grades.

All of his teachers at that time were women; indeed, throughout his schooling prior to Harvard, the main educational influence was from women. It was an English teacher, a woman, who insisted that he apply to Harvard, even though very few students in the school had ever done so.

Otherwise, his boyhood was uneventful and unmarred by tragedies or traumatic events. Life was regular and ordered, polite and supportive.

Jonathan's high school days were busy and exciting. He noted that the school emphasized extracurricular activities more than academic, and he threw himself into these with enthusiasm. He studied hardly at all, but was bright enough to receive honor grades anyway. He was involved in plays, in social clubs, in band trips, and in the duties of a class officer. He was popular with students and teachers alike and fitted into a group of about twenty or twenty-five boys and girls who ran the social life of the school. He was out of the house almost every weekend, either working at school, planning an event, or having a party at someone's house. The emphasis in his social life was on the group, and at their parties there was little pairing off or going steady. As he told it, there was also little emphasis on sexuality, because the social code forbade it and because they were so busy with other activities. There was never a dull moment socially, but Jonathan was not greatly inspired in intellectual matters, nor did he give much thought to what he would like to do with his life.

He spoke of the summer between high school and Harvard as boring and disillusioning; he had filled his empty days by getting records from the library and listening to music and by reading different things. There was some indication not only that he was sad about leaving high school but that he needed to be involved in many exciting events in order to cope with a tendency to depression. He thought a good deal about Harvard; it was Jonathan who had the fantasy that Harvard would be like Oxford of a hundred years ago. He seemed to be ready to leave for new experiences, much as he had shifted from home to school and community in his primary and secondary school years.

The Early Harvard Years: Plays and People

An account of Jonathan's Harvard experience breaks quite naturally into two sections on the basis of his activity patterns and his reaction

to environmental events. In the freshman and sophomore years his activities centered around the theater, but after some difficulties there
he became more introverted in his last two years and much less involved in organized extracurricular activities.

One of the main reasons Jonathan had selected Harvard in preference to other Ivy League schools was the freshman seminar program, and one of the high points of his freshman year, and indeed
of his four years at Harvard, was a seminar in creative writing. His
instructor became his ideal, a man who seemed to know practically
everything on a subject, who explained things clearly and who gave
students the feeling of his caring and concern for them as individuals.
Jonathan walked and talked with him, much as he had with his grandfather, and the seminar was thus much more than an academic exercise. His interest in writing or teaching as a career, particularly in
writing plays, emerged during this year and stayed with him in one
form or another through his time at Harvard.

During these first two years Jonathan selected most of his courses
from literature, music, and foreign languages, but in order to fulfill his academic requirements he took two courses in the general
education program, one on the history of ideas and one in the
natural sciences. Here he had difficulty and was not able to draw
the honor grades that had always come to him in the past. In general, he felt that his thinking was not too well organized, that if he
took the time for organization the courses would become boring.
In his social science course, the section man told him that he tended to personalize his papers too much by using his own experiences
and colloquial expressions—too much use of his personality and
not enough conceptualization. In these courses, he was not as clear
as he should have been and did not document things with sufficient
carefulness. This cognitive style is important to keep in mind in
view of other evidence we shall cite shortly from the Rorschach.

Jonathan's involvement with his teachers remained intensive during these two years. He spoke with particular admiration of his
instructor in a course on Shakespeare, describing him as an inspiring
man who, despite his shy and nervous manner, could be classed
among the "great" teachers.

The most pleasure seemed to come, however, from extracurricular activities. Jonathan played in orchestras, took part in plays, and
devoted time to writing for his own pleasure. In his freshman interviews he talked a great deal about activities at the Loeb Theater; it

obviously attracted him and represented many of the things he wanted. He found the people in drama enticing because of the freedom in their way of living, at the same time disturbing because of the departure they represented from the traditional values of Southern Baptists.

In the fall term of sophomore year, he directed a play with some degree of success and satisfaction. In the spring he decided to direct another. After he had assembled the cast with a great deal of difficulty and had begun rehearsals, the leading lady abandoned him and the play and other cast members became ill. The result was a chaotic situation in which he felt helpless and unable to exert control. He grew a bit philosophical when he commented that it was frustrating because "we, in the twentieth century, believe we can control anything." When he described this incident in the interview, he went on to speak about his boredom and about his disillusionment with society. He felt there was no place to escape, no place to hide, in the modern world: "You can't run away any longer. You have to face your problems and find out what they are. You never can go faster than the speed of light. And that's a big shock. I don't know when I heard that . . . age twelve or something . . . you can only go so far . . . and now you've got to accept that . . . we can't just romanticize . . . and that's growing up I guess."

Apparently the injury to Jonathan's self-esteem, as well as the realistic complications of the situation, unleashed a flood of feeling that he displaced onto social issues and the solar system. But at the same time there were hints in his words about a new perspective concerning limitation on us all and on his ability in particular. But another blow was yet to come; the play went on but received a devastating review. Though shaken by this series of events, he did not panic, did not leave school or go into a deep depression; instead, he picked up the pieces and finished the year with a good academic record. But the effects lasted through the rest of his Harvard years.

He began writing a play early in his sophomore year, and the topic was of particular interest because he chose as his subject a historical character from a humble background who deserted his family, expounded a doctrine of salvation based on repentence of sin, and at the same time expressed a powerful sexual attractiveness and the ability to exert great power over both the Church and the nobility. Jonathan often talked about his desire to say something important through a play and hinted that he had fantasies about possessing a special talent and would be someone with a great, noble spirit. This harked back to his grammar school days, when his teachers first indicated that he might be different and somewhat special. But, even though Jonathan worked on this play off and on during the year, he never finished it and after his sophomore year never mentioned it again.

A third area to describe in his early college years is that of interpersonal relationships. We noted that he had a host of friends in high school and apparently expected that he could find the same situation at Harvard. Indeed, he met and interacted with many people from both Harvard and Radcliffe. He took trips with them, discussed things over coffee at the "Bick," visited their homes, worked on plays, and went to movies and concerts with them. He dated some, though the relationships seemed to be intellectual more than sexual and he did not develop a serious relationship with any girl. One of his peers did have an impact on him, his freshman roommate, a highly intelligent and talented student named Paul. They came from quite different backgrounds. Paul was inclined to be brusque or rude to people if he did not like them and was more free and open about both his aggressive and sexual impulses. Jonathan did not quite know how to take Paul; he disliked him for what he considered to be boorishness and yet at the same time was attracted to him for his genuine openness. He also recognized a similarity between Paul and himself, which he described as follows: "I see in Paul things which I know are in me and I don't admire them, and for that reason I am kind of put off by a lot of things he does. Both of us are the kind of people that need for people to say to us that we are pretty good before we feel secure. But he does go about it in a different way and it is a way that really hurts other people, I think." Unfortunately, Paul was forced to leave Harvard after freshman year because of financial difficulties, but the two kept in touch by letter.

About his other friends, Jonathan often commented that he had to be on his guard with them, that they were too serious, and that there was too much intellectual one-upmanship going on. He tried his joking behavior with them only to find that they took him seriously. Thus, he could never quite relax and be himself. We have already noted his fascination with the drama group and his reluc-

tance to become too involved because he was not sure he could sub-
scribe to their values.

Much as in his years in high school, Jonathan's interpersonal relationships at college were mostly with groups and mostly on a level
that precluded intimacy or real emotional involvement. This is one
of the reasons why Paul disturbed him, because Paul challenged him
on the realness of his relationships. Jonathan once admitted that he
was not sure he had ever had a really close friend.

Finally, there are interesting data in the projective tests that help
us understand Jonathan's personality in these first two years. A number of features made his Rorschach protocol unique. He gave a large
number of responses and gave them quickly, one after the other, as
fast as the examiner could write them down in shorthand. Furthermore, he concentrated on small and tiny details, on the edges of the
blots or inside them. A large proportion of his responses were scored
as "originals," and many of these were of good form content. He
appeared to be trying to overwhelm the examiner with his respon-
siveness and to be unusual and clever about it at the same time. He
gave relatively few responses to the whole blot or to large usual details, which led Dr. McArthur to comment that he might experience
difficulty in courses requiring a broad conceptual grasp of problems.
That was exactly what happened in his social science course. Dr.
McArthur also felt that his protocol betrayed a defense by percep-
tual vigilance and that he tended to intellectualize and not empathize. He found evidence for some inner agitation and sensed the
presence of problems in sexual identification of which Jonathan
was probably unaware. Dr. McArthur felt that Jonathan would not
easily let others see through his protective armor of intellectual-
ism and cleverness. He also saw strengths in the record: adequate
perception of reality and control mechanisms, superior intelligence, and sufficient creativity so that he might do very well in the
field of literature. The key factors for our present account, however, were his difficulty in broad conceptual thinking and his
defense against the intrusion of others into his inner self. We can see
now that his bustling extracurricular activity and the writing of
plays and stories provided an outlet for his talents and brought emotional income, but in it he did not allow anyone to get very close to
him.

The picture becomes more complete if we bring in data from his freshman Thematic Apperception Test. His stories were full of descriptive detail but had little about the feelings of the characters. Strong emotions were muted, either by the actions of the characters or because such emotions occurred in dreams or under unusual circumstances. Women people his plots more than men, but there seemed to be ambivalence about them; at times they were portrayed as gossipy and naive, at times as devious and aggressive, at times as nurturant. His male heroes were not powerful figures, but neither were they at the mercy of fate or of women. Thus, we find strengths in this record in the well-constructed and detailed plots, with their sense of reality and characters who handled situations without falling to pieces. We also find that he defended against deep feelings by superficial detail and that there was some confusion about his sexual identity and his relationship to women.

Summers at Home

The summers between Jonathan's Harvard years constitute a crucial part of our case history and are probably more important in understanding the development of our subject than was true in the first three cases we have presented. He went home each year and worked for the local newspaper as a general reporter and feature writer. Three things impressed us from these summer experiences: the growing feeling that he had little in common with the round of life at home, even though he felt a sense of security there; the happiness, and then later the gradual pulling apart, that he experienced with his peer group; and the excitement and disillusionment with society that he found from behind the scenes at the newspaper.

After freshman year, the summer was the best he had ever known. He spoke with enthusiasm of seeing his old friends and comparing college experiences with them. The mixed peer group was off every weekend on trips, or picnics, or mixed slumber parties (that were quite asexual). He delighted in telling us how different this was from the boy-girl relationships he saw in Cambridge. The tenor of his description, however, indicated that there was much going about and a great deal of talk, but little deep emotional involvement.

In the summer after sophomore year, Jonathan underwent considerable change. He felt a growing distance from his former friends and from his family. As to the latter, he said it was great to be with them, but he also made it clear that he could no longer communicate with them on the level of his interests. They did not make demands on him, however, or interfere with his activities, but neither did they give him anything in the way of direction.

The major disillusionment came at the newspaper, when he was confronted by the evidence that highly respected citizens not only committed crimes but succeeded in avoiding both newspaper publicity and police charges by using influence, financial as well as social. He now recognized that he had had "illusions about people." He said: "It turns out that everybody in a position of prominence has done something bad . . . that you'd rather not know about." He also learned that money talks. So his idealism became further undermined by confrontation with the phenomenon of crime and hypocrisy. He longed once again for a "class of nobles . . . good people, high-minded and respectable people." Since he had begun to doubt that his wish would come true and to realize that all men are capable of both good and evil, some degree of social consciousness dawned, but as yet it found no outlet in action.

The Latter Years: Career Questions and Increasing Introversion

Jonathan was not at all certain that he wanted to come back to Harvard for his junior year, primarily because he was not sure about what he would do after he graduated. Up to this point he had thought about combining a career in teaching and writing, but he now realized that he had real doubts about going to graduate school. He wanted to have time and freedom to write, but that idea scared him because he might get drafted. He said: "Suppose you go six to eight years and don't amount to anything, and you decide, well, I'm going to be, and then you don't know what you're going to be. It's a big risk to take." He wanted to travel but thought he would have to go into the army first and would be old and bored when he got out. The idea of being a "bum" and not caring what people thought about him appeared in his conversations. Graduate school would provide security for the future and protect him from the draft, but his ideas about teaching were now undergoing change. He said that he used to be idealistic about teaching but felt that it was difficult to combine teaching and writing, especially at a place like Harvard. He also said, "In some places you teach and you teach and you teach and nobody cares and I'm too selfish to do that without people caring." We wondered if he was beginning to make a more valid comparison between his own intellectual potential and that of the upper echelon at Harvard and to make a more realistic assessment of his own creative ability. This may have been behind his reluctance about graduate school. At any rate, the interviews in his last two years were notable for the frequent discourses about travel, writing, being a bum, graduate school as a haven but also a dead end, and the desire to say something important to the world. Jonathan was confused and did not have any clear ideas of what to do.

At the same time he cut back on his participation in extracurricular activities. He said that he planned it that way and wanted more time to enjoy studying; he wondered if all the time he had put into outside things had been worth it. Thus, he spent more time in the library and read more and received honors grades in his courses in English.

Although he entered more fully into the academic life, he also found a growing disillusionment with some of his teachers. He was distressed by the "nervousness" and "competitiveness" of the faculty members and said that he had been saddened by reports he heard of the loneliness and poignancy of one favorite teacher's personal life. He felt that some professors played politics too much and were reluctant to speak up on things because they were afraid they might make fools of themselves. Whereas he had earlier glorified the role of the university professor, he now spoke of the academic as a "very scary grind." And with this thought came a feeling of anxiety about competing with the Harvard faculty on their own level.

With the gradual decathexis of the old identification figures, two new heroes began to assume importance: an outstanding European film director and Joseph Conrad. The former appealed to him because he had a wonderful sense of humanity and characters, was humorous, seemed to be doing something even though apparently disorganized, and was flamboyant. As for Conrad, he was attracted by the fact that at forty Conrad turned to writing books, wonderful and important books, that told about life and were beautifully written. Conrad started anew at midlife, in a new language, and Jonathan felt he would like a similar emotional experience. His interest in these two heroes suggested that just as he had sought and found a better home away from home when he was an adolescent, so now he was seeking a better home away from Harvard by his junior year.

It is not surprising that at the same time his restlessness increased and he used Harvard as a point of departure for more and more trips. The biggest adventure came in the spring of his junior year, when he went home for vacation with Paul, his freshman roommate. In addition to the aura of the much-traveled man that Paul exuded, he had a flamboyant family, and the trip served the added factor of bringing Jonathan back toward the theater, with which Paul's father was involved. Also, the relationship with Paul was renewed, and it led to the closest friendship Jonathan had at Harvard. Later on, when he described this trip, he spoke of it as "running away," and his association to this was running away from the extracurricular activities of his previous two years. He felt that he would have enjoyed the "extracurricular thing" a little more had people been less nervous and tense about it. People in the theater at Harvard gave their whole time to it and went through all sorts of emotional crisis. They were unhappy, he felt, though exciting to be with; there should have been release from tension in that activity, and just the reverse was true. Getting away from Harvard helped him get away from those unpleasant memories.

He could not dismiss extracurricular activities completely. For part of one year he taught a course in creative writing in a prison. Here too, though, he was somewhat disillusioned; he found the people boring. Also, the one person in his class who had any ability kept talking about a play he was going to write but never did anything about it. Perhaps the most valuable part of the experience was his surprise at the "unprisonlike" atmosphere; he wondered if it was much of a punishment to be confined there. We could only speculate, but we wondered if this exposure to the reality of prison life, in contrast to his fantasies about the wages of sin, together with his exposure to the realities of social crime during the previous summer, might have had some modifying effect on Jonathan's rather harsh superego.

He also had one more fling at the stage. During the summer after his junior year, he worked on another play. The theme was integration between the races, a topic he had avoided up to this point. He

approached it by using both white and black actors and making a
comedy out of it, casting extremists on both sides as the villains
and white and black moderates as heroes. He tried to cast it in his
senior year and asked the same girl who had disappointed him as
leading lady in his sophomore year to play one of the heroines.
The same results were forthcoming; she deserted him again. This
time he took it with greater equanimity, perhaps because he had
grown older in the interim, or was more inured to it because of
the previous experience, or was not as emotionally committed
and dependent on the theater group. The play was never produced,
and that was as far as Jonathan went on the problem of integration.

As he grew away from participation in theater activities, he also
narrowed his circle of friends and pulled more into himself. During
his last two years, there was much less running about, fewer big
parties, and more willingness to be critical of people. For example,
he found his roommates to be more conservative than he liked, and
he had less and less in common with them as time went on. Also,
he did not get close to any of the numerous girls he knew. He had
always had a crush on a long-time friend at home but he now had
to accept the fact that she was heading off into a career of her own
and to recognize that his fantasies about a life with her would have
to be replaced by something different. He said that he had always
been attracted to tall, slender, graceful women with prominent facial
features, often a little older than he was. He volunteered that he
might have an affair with one in the next year or two but did not
contemplate marriage for a while. He admitted that his attitudes
toward premarital intercourse had undergone some change and that
he was no longer against it. This change in attitude had not yet been
accompanied by change in behavior, and the idea of an affair was
still fantasy.

Our account for his last two years may come through as somewhat
disorganized or disjointed, but the flow of ideas in his interviews was
even more so. He was changing, ambivalent and confused, but as
yet had resolved little. One event in his senior year may have been
a symptom of the confusion and of his search for answers and provides an interesting sidelight on his development. For a year or so
he had been intrigued by the new use of hallucinogenic drugs, which
were just coming into vogue, and finally resolved to try one himself.
He chose peyote, thinking that the visual distortions would be fun

because of his interest in art forms and perceptually altered physical states. His cognitive style was particularly good for describing such an event, and that particular interview section is a classic description of a drug reaction. His "trip" lasted longer than he had anticipated, a little over twenty-four hours, and produced some unexpected reactions on his part. It began quite benignly, with some distortion of time perspective and alteration of visual boundaries. As the evening wore on, objects began to assume unusual shapes, and colors became an ever-moving panorama. He had taken the drug with a friend, who was also under the influence of peyote, and they spent some time walking around the Square and to museums. Jonathan took considerable care on this excursion to stay away from close friends, especially Paul, his earlier roommate, because he did not want them to see him in an "unnatural" state. By midnight and the early hours of the morning, he wanted to sleep but could not, and as everyone else in the House eventually went to bed, he was left alone. He was terrified, in much the same way that some little children are afraid of dark closets, and stayed by the window waiting an eternity for the first light of dawn to come.

After describing the drug experience in his interview, he went into a long series of associations about his relationships with people. He began with the reaction he had to Paul and the admission to himself, under the effect of the peyote, of all the things he did not like about Paul. His next association was that when he lost control of his emotions he got hurt, and he did not like that. This was the reason he gave up acting. He wanted to find a woman that he could love, wanted to find a relationship where he could express himself freely without being hurt. He said that under the effects of peyote he had come to the conclusion that he was meant to be alone.

Apparently the drug experience broke down his defenses to the extent that some of his basic fears about his aggression and about his worthlessness came close to consciousness. We could not tell how successfully he was going to be in dealing with this material or how he might alter his defensive stance, if at all. He said he would like to try the experience again, although apparently he did not while at Harvard.

The experience with peyote apparently was one representation of his conflict about the kind of controls he should impose on his impulses and about the kind of defenses he used to combat his loneliness and anxiety. The superego of his Southern Baptist days was changing, and the activity patterns of high school days were changing. He was becoming both more introverted and freer in his impulse expression, yet that process was a painful and confusing one for him. We could not predict the outcome of these matters with much confidence, but we did think that by now he was in a better position to confront important issues within himself than he had been before.

Jonathan said little in his senior interviews about his honors thesis. Clearly, it did not have the personal meaning for him that it did for Jason Jellinec or the instrumental implications that it did for Joseph Kramer. Jonathan regarded his tutor as competent, but he did not identify with him or interact with him as he had with the man who taught his freshman seminar. Although he wrote an excellent thesis and graduated *magna cum laude,* he gave the impression in the interviews that in some manner the thesis was a task of secondary importance to him at that stage of his life; he was involved with it, yet there were other, more important, things on his mind.

He did make one comment about his thesis topic that revealed his struggle for internal meaning and structure. The topic of his thesis was the analysis of some novels of a late-nineteenth-century American author, and Jonathan noted that this man had the capacity to catch the entire meaning of things in a phrase or sentence and to make that meaning crystal clear. Jonathan was intrigued with this skill, perhaps because in his own state of mind he longed to be able to do the same thing and in a flash of insight to solve his own confusion.

In the last interview, he volunteered a comparison of his grammar school and his high school years with his college experience. His high school life, he said, corresponded to the first two years at Harvard; his grammar school years, in an interesting way, more nearly resembled his last two years at college.

> The similarities being that in grammar school I went to the library a lot and read, and I lost all that, or a great deal of it, by entering an active life in high school. My affections for high school I'll never forget, and probably because that was the one time when I really went completely out for this sort of active life. Hardly read anything those last two years . . . never

a moment not spent in planning some project or administering like a businessman, you know, or getting votes, or doing something of that sort. Well, I'm kind of happy not to be doing that, and here there is no pressure to do that, and had I gone to college at home, I might have tried to do that for no reason. So, the nice thing about Harvard is that it has let me become what I wanted to be . . . free to do what I wanted to, no social pressure. It has great people, too, in the undergraduate college, and I'm glad to have met many of them. They're independent, and they aren't . . . they aren't as friendly as people seem to be at other places, but they are wonderful people in their own right and they've been very pleasant to know.

He had referred to his parents, too, as wonderful, but he had left them behind. He was bidding goodbye to Harvard and adolescence as he had to childhood and family, his former teachers, and his old friends, despite the fact that it was "scary" to leave them and go forth into the unknown world. Jonathan had made his choice. Though his course was essentially uncharted, he was at least future-oriented for the first time in his college career.

As graduation approached, he decided to go abroad and planned to enroll in a university to maintain his student status. But mainly he wanted to travel, to meet new people, perhaps to have an affair, and to write, outside the restraints of home or college.

Personality Change during College

When we consider the social and cultural difference between the easy, comfortable, close-knit life of Virginia from whence Jonathan came and the cosmopolitan, highly individual life around Harvard and Boston, we might expect that the discordance would lead to behavioral and attitudinal changes of some magnitude and perhaps to underlying personality modification. Harvard upheld other standards and values than those to which he had been accustomed, represented other mores. Its faculty and students also spoke "another language." In spite of this, Jonathan did not change greatly. It is true that there was some perceptible growth, and Jonathan, like his classmate Jason Jellinec, could not go home again, but the changes were primarily of the kind that set the stage for later personality modification.

His status can be ascertained best by reviewing the changes, or lack thereof, on our six variables. Jonathan had a capacity for *object relations* that was evident in his host of friendships at home and the ease with which he met people. He was part of a triumvirate including another boy and a girl, which had existed since the first grade; thus his relationships could be sustained. In high school they did everything together and were among the center group of social leaders. The friendship continued into college, and Jonathan carried on an active correspondence with them while he was at Harvard. Beyond these two, he had many other friends and seemed to be universally liked. He formed a close relationship at Harvard with Paul, a man who could be rude and abrasive at times. Also, he was able to identify with adults, as with the man who taught his freshman seminar.

There was, however, a limited quality to his object relations that may have been associated with his growing tendency to spin in upon himself as he went through Harvard. We must remember that a close friend told him that people at Harvard would not catch on to him, because it had taken them many years at home to do so. His friends apparently thought that he had difficulty in being open and close. Dr. McArthur concluded from his Rorschach protocols that there was an underlying difficulty with empathy and acceptance of others. We also must remember that relationships with his family were limited. He said that his parents were wonderful, but he could not identify with his father or share with his parents more than talk about family, community, and friends. Although he had two younger sisters, he never mentioned them in his interviews after the family interview of the freshman year. Finally, his feelings about Paul were jolted during the peyote experience, when Jonathan realized the extent of his hostility toward Paul.

The pattern of interaction in high school, which was characterized by constant activity and where the emphasis was on shared activity rather than shared feelings, was not appropriate either for Harvard or for young adulthood. This realization forced Jonathan to reassess his relations with people, and the disillusionment and turning away from people that occurred in college was probably a necessary step if more empathic and intimate object relations were to occur eventually. Whereas our first three cases had moved steadily toward capacity for intimacy, Jonathan was just becoming aware of factors in himself that could interfere with closeness.

His experience in school and the community at home was of the kind to sustain high *self-esteem.* He was well regarded by his teachers and classmates, was in the center of school activities, had ample opportunity to use his varied talents, and received many honors. There was no indication that he was burdened by guilt or self-denigration. It was in his sophomore year at college that the first serious blows to his self-esteem occurred, when people deserted him as he tried to cast a play and when his efforts were faulted in a review. Thus, in the last two years there was more self-doubt than he had experienced before. Again, we may have witnessed a change that was necessary before a more mature self-esteem could be derived, one that was based more on internal assurance than on the acclaim of others. Until the sophomore year, people for the most part had been uncritical about Jonathan, and some realistic correction was perhaps in order. In his last two years, he began the task of searching out what he was good for, and in his fascination with being a bum, he may have been saying that he wanted to be free of judgment until he could evaluate himself and his talents more accurately. Again, there is a contrast with our previous cases; each of them had graduated with a feeling of self-esteem that was more secure than when they had entered Harvard.

Our initial contacts with Jonathan indicated that he had few *mood* swings and that his predominate mood was happy and accepting of people. Although he indicated that this was in part a reflection of the Southern style of interpersonal friendliness and agreeability, we had reason to believe that he had incorporated it into his personality. Some dysphoria did appear during college: in the depression he went through following the disaster with his play, when he referred to his trip with Paul in his junior year as "running away," and when he came to the realization under the effects of peyote that he was destined to be alone. His senior Rorschach protocol also contained evidence of dysphoria, whereas there had been none in freshman year. His depressions were not as acute, however, as those experienced by Joseph Kramer, nor did he feel the need to ward off depression as did Kramer.

His stability of mood was a marked feature of his college experience, especially in view of the psychopathology on his father's side of the family. It was a hopeful sign that he might be able to change his adaptive techniques in the years after college. We must remember that there was good reason for his depression in his sophomore year and also that it did not interfere with superior academic achievement.

His *interest patterns* were bounded by literature and music. He had little or no attraction to sports, to things mechanical, or to the world of business, although he did say at one time that politics intrigued him. He was also oriented toward occupations that served people, and on the Strong Vocational Interest Blank he had high scores on Group VI, the so-called social service scales, much as did Jason Jellinec. However, he had "reject" patterns on the science and many of the professional scales and on occupations that often involve outdoor manual labor. Thus, he had clear-cut and definite interest patterns, in contrast to the flat profile that characterized Joseph Kramer. His scores on the Strong changed little in four years aside from increases in the verbal scales like author-journalist, and his desire to be a writer of some kind continued unabated. He did give up thoughts of teaching, but whether this was from lack of interest or fear of competition, we could not say for sure. Jonathan's interests became more certain during college, but at graduation there was still a question as to whether he could fulfull them to his satisfaction, that is, whether he could be a successful writer.

Goal-directed behavior did not mesh with interest patterns to the extent that it did in our first three cases. Other than wanting to "say something important," Jonathan was confused about his goals. He spoke of wanting to be a bum but did not seem to know how this would help him achieve anything; and indeed, this seemed more of an escape reaction than a goal-directed one. There was confusion and unease in this aspect of his personality, to a greater extent than we observed in most of the subjects in our total interview sample.

We can speculate about a number of sources for his problem. He had little direction from his parents; they were inclined to leave things up to him and accede to his wishes. Although there was some passivity in their natures, we also must realize that they knew little of the world into which he was going and therefore lacked the knowledge to give him direction.

At the same time, he was accommodating to a value system that was at variance with the Southern Baptist tradition. He acknowledged in his senior year that he had not been emotionally involved with religion since his early teen years and that he went to church more out of convention than anything else. His scores on some of our tests for values showed that he tended toward emergent rather than traditional values; that is, there was an emphasis on sociability rather than individuality, present time orientation rather than future, and a being orientation rather than hard work. The acceptance of the emergent position increased while he was at Harvard. We do not argue that his confusion stemmed from adherence to emergent values, but rather that these were sufficiently different from the milieu in which he was reared to cause ambivalence and conflict. His desire to be a bum might give him the time and freedom to resolve that conflict, but that was a future task and not one that was handled in college, as our other subjects had done.

On the matter of control, we have noted that Jonathan had a rather strict superego when he matriculated and that he kept both sexual and aggressive impulses under close rein. The Rorschach indicated that his natural tendency was to be impulsive, but apparently he was able to limit that to joking and having fun, to going on trips at the spur of the moment. These behaviors were supported by his social group at home, and there was some opportunity, although less support, for doing those things at Harvard.

Contact with Paul, with the drama crowd at the Loeb, and with people from all walks of life helped Jonathan in easing his superego demands and freeing his impulses. We have commented on his professed interest in having an affair, his willingness to use a hallucinogenic drug, and his awareness of his underlying anger. Along with these new feelings, there was also more anxiety by senior year, shown in his Rorschach and on a manifest anxiety scale. Although his defensive posture against uncomfortable feelings was much the same, more of them now came through. In this regard, he was like most of the students we studied, and certainly like the first three we described.

One of Jonathan's primary ways of managing tension was a technique we observed in Joseph Kramer, that of change of place. He did not do it with the same conscious intent as did Kramer, but the net result was the same. His numerous trips away from Harvard, often on the spur of the moment, helped him handle anxiety that came from too close involvement or feelings of self-doubt that came from potential rejection. Also he was a compromiser, as he put it, which provided a way of blunting affect that might otherwise have been overwhelming, especially anger. The former technique, change of place, worked well all the time he was at Harvard; the latter, compromising, became less effective as it was challenged by some of his friends, especially Paul.

Jonathan had the capacity to direct and utilize his energies and could work effectively. His honor-grade academic work attested to that, as did his extracurricular involvement. He said that he enjoyed directing plays because of the opportunity it gave him to control people and events toward a desired end. Two things limited his capacity: his cognitive style and the difficulty he had in finishing things when not under pressure. Cognitively, he was not a conceptualizer, and he appeared to have some awareness of that when he admitted that he was not good at critical writing. We might expect he would have difficulty in being philosophical or in dealing with major human issues in his writing. This issue he had not faced fairly as he left Harvard. As to the motivation for work, we noted that he started a number of plays without finishing them. In his senior year he complained that one danger of the freedom at Harvard was in not forcing people to do things, and he felt he needed to be forced. It is interesting to speculate whether or not Jonathan might have staying power with work if he could come to terms with his inner nature and not have to spend so much energy in being vigilant. On that score, we felt inadequate in looking into the future.

Chapter 8 / Hugh Post

The following comments were made by an astute physician when Hugh Post came in for a physical examination at the beginning of his freshman year:

> Comes in with a rather amused, condescending, bored manner, as one who is tolerating a nuisance. I gather this reflects his relationship in general and manner of approaching college. Probably will come into some conflict because of his approach. I get the impression that underneath he is rather unhappy and rather immature. Probably rather bright and this will enhance his chances of success. Motivation is questionable. His remarks on depression, which he minimizes, trouble me a little. I anticipate difficulty in college and career.

The doctor had not met Hugh before and knew nothing about him; his only information came from Hugh's behavior in the examination.

Another physician described Hugh on a different occasion, over a year later: "Steady, friendly, courteous, and pleasant fellow. Is doing better this time around." The difference in tone of the observations could have been affected by personality variations in the two doctors, both in the reactions they drew from Hugh and in their readiness to perceive him in particular ways. But we think more was involved and that the contrast in characterization reflected something in Hugh Post rather than in the two physicians. The weight of our evidence from interviews and psychological tests indicated that both men were correct. Post did have conflict and difficulty in his freshman year, was an unhappy man very often, and, as he later admitted, was also immature. He was sufficiently unhappy in that year to withdraw from Harvard for awhile, returning only after a period of travel and work abroad. On the second time around, he had confronted certain conflicts within himself and was making some progress on the growth tasks of forming a stable identity and improving his object relations, in contrast to his previous narcissism. We do not mean to imply that the shift was dramatic and that he was a changed person; Hugh would not have liked that, nor would that have been a likely outcome within his particular character structure. He does, however, illustrate a pattern where there is an interruption in development through a crisis and where the evidence for a reintegrative process is visible before the student finishes college. This was not a common pattern among our subjects, but it happened with a few. We present the case not only to demonstrate a particular pattern, but also to force us to look at adaptation and continuity under unusual circumstances.

Family and School Background

One of the most formative influences in Hugh's early years was the relationship he had with his maternal grandparents. They were talented and educated people; his grandfather spoke half a dozen languages, read widely, and designed buildings. His grandmother painted, took courses at the nearby university, and was an avid reader. Hugh spent a lot of time with them during his childhood because his parents made extended visits to various parts of the country in connection with his father's business. Hugh said that they taught him to read before he went to kindergarten, a fact which perhaps says something about Hugh's intelligence as well as their efforts. He regarded his grandmother as a woman of warmth and understanding, who in his later years seemed to be the only one who had confidence that he would eventually sort things out for himself. She provided the emotional warmth, while his grandfather nourished his young intellect. The grandfather was limited in his emotional contribution by his personality characteristics, which Hugh described as contentious; apparently he was not able to get along well with people, and this became worse as he grew older. He was "brilliant but neurotic." Nonetheless, Hugh liked the old man and in the interviews always spoke of both grandparents with respect.

Hugh's feelings about his parents were less positive. In spite of her background, he regarded his mother as someone who had little to say that was worthwhile and who did not seem to have much faith in his ability to grow up. During all of his childhood, she either had worked or had traveled with his father on some of his numerous business trips.

The elder Post was an interesting person who had held a number of different jobs, most of which were entrepreneurial and which involved sales schemes he had in mind. Although he was imaginative and enthusiastic, he rarely succeeded in keeping an idea viable to the conclusion of great financial success. Hugh said that "the money comes in gallons and goes out in bushels," and that the family was chronically in debt as his father promoted one venture after another. Hugh seemed to be attracted by his father's imagination and initiative but unsettled by his inability to stay at one thing and make it successful.

His account suggested some parental discord; he talked about "battles" that arose out of his mother's concern for the precarious financial situation. He also implied that his father liked to fancy himself attractive to women, but he never spoke of his father as having affairs and did not indicate that his parents had contemplated divorce.

Although there was some moving around when Hugh was a baby, the family settled near a large city on the west coast, were joined by the maternal grandparents, and Hugh spent all his life there until he came to Harvard. His paternal grandfather was dead, his paternal grandmother lived abroad, and there were no other relatives mentioned by him in accounting for his childhood adolescence.

Hugh was sent to parochial school, even though his family was not Roman Catholic, because it was the only school in the community with a full-day activity program. He took to the schooling and the religion with some enthusiasm, and for a period of time he went to Mass quite frequently and said that he was very religious. This feeling waned as he moved into adolescence, and although he continued in the parochial school system, he did so with increasing unease. Indeed, the onset of adolescence appeared to be a time of considerable change in terms of his interests and the outlets for his abilities. He had an early introduction to heterosexual activity; by age fifteen he had started writing madly, usually novels; and he read anything he could lay his hands on. Along with this he stopped going to Mass and soon began to question things openly in the classroom, especially some of the teaching of the Church. He said that during this part of his adolescence he was a great romantic, and his telling of it suggested that he was an exuberant as well as a loquacious one.

Hugh moved over to the public high school in his city, where there was greater intellectual freedom but where the life style of the students appalled him. He compared them with a bunch of thugs, and spoke disparagingly of their duck-tail hair styles and their leather jackets, their lack of interest in things intellectual or aesthetic, and their unpredictable aggressiveness. He did not speak of any friends among the student body or of any sustained activity in social activities.

We found it difficult to weigh Hugh's report for accuracy. The picture of his high school seemed overdrawn and could have been partly a product of his highly critical and belittling manner. On the other hand, some city and suburban high schools were then, and still are, comparable to blackboard jungles. His reaction could also have been affected by his high intelligence and what he felt to be lack of intellectual stimulation. For example, he commented that he was always bothered by the fact that his high school mathematics courses never went far enough: "They always stopped with the binomial theory." Most courses he felt to be without challenge, even stultifying in their effect. Only one teacher came close to meeting Hugh's standards, and the two of them had a very open and intellectually honest relationship. He urged Hugh to apply to Berkeley, the University of Chicago, or Harvard.

His grades were high, nearly all A's in spite of the fact that he studied very little and took extra courses. He implied that getting honor grades was something he could do "with his left hand" while he was at the same time writing novels and listening to music.

Post's friends through the years seemed to be few in number. He spoke of one boy who lived nearby and whom he felt close to, of another who was a few years his senior and taught him about music, and of a girl with whom he went steady. The latter was the closest peer relationship he had and one that he portrayed as involving constancy on the part of the girl, whom we shall call Phyllis, and somewhat less than wholehearted participation on his part. He said that she was extremely beautiful and madly in love with him, but he also said that she was not his intellectual equal and that he could not contemplate a whole life with her. He implied that the relationship meant a great deal to him but that he was not ready to commit himself to anybody.

One other aspect of his object relations is important in this background section. He said that when his parents were away for extended periods he would usually find a "substitute family," in spite of the fact that he was staying with his grandparents. He described one such incident and indicated that he went over to the other house after breakfast and did not come home again until bedtime, every day! As he told it, he indicated that it was a kind of total involvement with the other family, as though he were a regular member, and an involvement at his initiative rather than theirs.

He came to Harvard with the idea that it was the only place to go; if one wanted to be an engineer one went to M.I.T. or Cal. Tech, otherwise, one went to Harvard. Thus, we might expect that he had some "great expectations" about the intellectual excitement and challenge he might find there in contrast to the "mediocre faculty, intolerable student body, imbecile courses, and undistinguished and absurd library" of his high school.

Freshman Year: A Growing Crisis

Hugh began his Harvard career with great activity. He signed up for extra courses, found a job to help with expenses, and began practicing the piano again as he had done in childhood. In addition, he spent a lot of time listening to music, reading, and writing letters to friends. He reported that his room was great, the food was fine, the library facilities were excellent, and the "professors have something to say." Many topics that become the source of student complaints were thus seen by him in a favorable light.

Yet, in the same first interview, early in October, he said that he was not very happy, although he did not know why. At another point in the interview, he said that although he enjoyed learning, it had occurred to him that he might quit unless there was some great turn of events, because Harvard was expensive and involved and he did not know if he was getting that much out of it. By midwinter he had become more critical, bitter, and lonely, and by spring he had decided to leave Harvard. He no longer liked his roommate; repeatedly during the year he had been disappointed with people; studies and academic life were no longer foremost in his mind; he was discouraged about his writing; and he felt his eyesight was deteriorating under the impact of constant reading. He said he "now had complete disgust for Harvard."

In order to understand this turn of events, it may be instructive to go over the year in more detail, looking both at aspects of his overt behavior and at certain clinical cues that we picked up concerning underlying dynamic issues.

Like Jonathan Thackery, Hugh signed up for a freshman seminar and similarly found himself with a teacher who cared for students and provided exciting intellectual interchange. Late in his freshman year, he looked back on this experience and said that he had learned an immense amount from this teacher, and that the man's greatest influence had come by "pointing out things that I am now hamstrung by as a writer," meaning that he had a florid style and could not sustain a theme through a number of situations in the plot. This experience was one of the bright spots of the year for him.

He also liked a French course, a new language for him. The level of expectation of the instructor was pitched high enough to make the course challenging for Hugh, and the teacher seemed enthusiastic about his job.

Also, on the positive side, he said that he found all his courses extremely easy. This he attributed in part to the fact that he had only to hear something once to remember it. As a consequence, he did not need to take notes or to underline or make notations in his books. He minimized his efforts by saying: "Yeah, I suppose what I do is called studying. It's not studying; it's just reading what's assigned to be read and writing what's assigned to be written and there's nothing extraordinary about it—there's no method."

At the same time, there were negative feelings about the academic side of his life. Concerning an astronomy course, he noted in the middle of the fall term that he had not yet heard anything he did not already know about the subject. He reserved most of his criticism and expressed most of his tension, however, toward his fellow students. For the first time he found people whom he considered his equals. He said that he had "gotten to the point now that I'm not so much above everything else and a few things in one respect or another are above me here." He also compared himself with his roommate, whom he regarded as a very intelligent person. It was only later that he could bring himself to tell us this, but he felt in the freshman year that his roommate, Gregory, was brighter, and that in subtle ways Gregory tended to belittle his ideas and his intelligence. Overtly, he told us that he did not know anybody who found the courses as easy as he did, but underneath he apparently felt a strong sense of intellectual competitiveness and had some doubts about how competent he really was.

As we reconstructed the process over the year, Hugh came with his high hopes and somewhat unrealistic expectations about intellectual challenge and inspiration and found initially that these were fulfilled. As the year progressed, his sense of competitiveness and self-doubt increased. He was conflicted about this and tried to reassure himself, and us, that he was as bright as any other students at Harvard, while at the same time he started to downgrade the value of education and its usefulness to him. Hugh was sufficiently intelligent so that most of his course grades were A or A−; thus his subjective opinion of himself was harsh and resulted in a need to prove himself better than anyone else. The basic struggle during freshman year was one of competitiveness and not really one of intellectual competence.

In the interpersonal area, it was apparent that Hugh felt doubly threatened by his roommate because the latter had a host of friends and seemed very adept at getting along with people. Gregory was well liked, whereas Hugh felt that other students turned to him either because his caustic remarks were entertaining or because he could help them with parts of their homework that they did not understand. As the year progressed, Hugh became more critical of Gregory: "My roommate and I are kind of . . . . it's just that we're an entirely different breed. We have very different attitudes toward everything. At first I was rather scared of him because he seemed to be such a success, and he was exactly the opposite of everything I had intended to carve out for myself. Now I'm just beginning to despise him." Later on, he said that Gregory talked at cross-purposes and tended to insert double meanings into what he said. Besides, he belittled things that Hugh did.

Hugh started pulling away from other students as well. On a number of occasions he spoke with some bitterness about students who were importunate, or noted that most students were too particular about their appearances. He said that he would really like to be one of the silent individuals who disdains everybody; in truth, that was what he was slowly becoming. In the fall term, he said, "we used to go in huge groups to dinner," but after mid-year exams he went alone or found a dinner companion from another dormitory. It is not surprising that in his spring interview he said that he was dissatisfied "with the whole idea of having to come here and everything."

Part of Hugh's difficulty was in his shyness, which he associated with hesitancy in meeting girls. He had become friendly with a Radcliffe student who was in one of his classes, but they seemed to have nothing more than a joking relationship. He missed Phyllis, and it was while talking about these matters that he said that his shyness was tied in with a fear of being rejected. He never learned to dance, because he would be afraid to ask girls to dance. He said, however, that "completely by accident, for some reason girls supplied themselves at intervals." But once again, it sounded like he was trying to convince us, and himself, of people's liking for him, when he really had some self-doubts about that.

Another part of Hugh's difficulty, like that of so many youths of his age, probably resided in his lack of certainty about his own sexual identity. He said that earlier in his adolescence he had wondered if he might have homosexual tendencies, and it is, therefore, not surprising that he should have some unease about the potential homosexual aspect of his relationship with Gregory and read into his roommate's conversation references to the subject.

The whole matter was complicated by the fact that he thought a graduate student was "working on having an affair" with him. Although no overt invitation was proferred for a sexual experience, the man invited Hugh to his rooms to "get tanked up on martinis" and was very friendly, "peculiarly friendly," as Hugh put it.

An interesting sidelight on his mounting anxiety came during the winter, when he decided, somewhat on the spur of the moment, to hitchhike to New York. He left with little money, which added to his sense of drama. "My idea was that I might get something to happen." It was a somewhat lonely trip, but one without any untoward incidents, and he returned tired but rather satisfied with himself. The trip may have served a number of purposes for him, not the least of which was a change of scene and thereby a lessening of tension. We had the feeling that there was also a counterphobic aspect to it, that is, that Hugh attempted to handle his anxiety about loneliness and rejection by putting himself in a situation where precisely that could occur. Subsequent behavior in our presentation of his case history makes that a tenable hypothesis, but further discussion of such defenses will come later.

Upon his return, his displeasure with the freshman year and with Harvard was heightened by the unpleasant aspects of his "work job." He had noted that his family was chronically in debt, and thus a good share of his expenses fell on his shoulders. Like many of his fellow students, he was given a job on the cleaning crew for the dormitories, a task he found boring and distasteful. We had other students in our sample who held the same job without experiencing the same negative reaction, and we wondered how much he might be transferring onto the job his anger at his father for not making better financial provisions for him. This was only speculation, because he gave no indication that there was such an association. At any rate, he was not a willing employee.

One tragedy did befall him during the year, the death of his beloved grandmother. He spoke to us not long after the event occurred, but did not accompany his news with a strong display of feeling. The appropriate feeling would have been sadness at the loss of the grandmother of whom he had been fond, but Post was keeping careful check on such emotions at this particular period in his life.

He did, however, feel a great deal of bitterness, despair, a kind of free-floating anxiety, and a strong need to get away from everything—Harvard, friends, and family. He did not exhibit any marked depression or acute panic, nor was he overwhelmed with anxiety, and he continued to do his academic work with distinction. He might not have called it a crisis; nevertheless, we considered that he was undergoing a crisis because his behavior was driven and there was evidence of considerable confusion, despite his ability to carry on in organized activities. It was not surprising that when the spring term ended, he dropped out of Harvard.

Freedom and Confrontation

For well over a year, Hugh was something of a vagabond, with no responsibilities to anyone, free to come and go as he wished and limited in what he did only by lack of money. In that period of time he hitchhiked all over the United States and Europe. He lived in Venice for a couple of months, and also in New York, but the greater part of the time he was on the road, staying in one place for a week or two, then moving on. He had a small amount of money that he had earned at home the summer after his freshman year, his father gave him a few hundred dollars, and he managed to pick up odd jobs along the way. His was no grand tour, yet he was not destitute.

The details of where he went and what he did are not crucial to our case presentation, but his style of life during that time and its meaning to him, as well as some critical incidents, are the focal points. When he began his journeys, he did so with the resolve that he would force a change in his personality; thus there was a certain amount of openness and willingness to learn from experience that we did not see at all in his freshman year at Harvard. The other general condition came from his vagabond status; that is, he was not in a competitive situation and did not feel the same pressure to impress people with his brilliance as he had heretofore. He did not need to get involved; he could observe, and when he wished he could move on to another place and new faces. The traveler often feels a certain freedom, as though he is not being watched and as though the rules and norms that ordinarily govern his life do not apply. Post felt this way and, consequently, his customary defenses could be relaxed a bit, thus allowing the possibility of confrontation and reorganization in his personality.

The major reshaping event occurred after he had been away from home for about six months and was staying in Rome for a few weeks. He met another American man, whom we shall call Bruce, a few years older than Hugh, whom Hugh admired greatly and who provided the one close interpersonal relationship of the year. He was able to talk with Bruce about his adventures with various people and also about some of his fears. He realized that he had never really opened his eyes to "find out what was really going on around me." That he could be obtuse to the real meaning of people's actions and their feelings was a revelation to him, and he spoke of this a number of times as he described his subsequent experiences.

Shortly after that he was confronted with his old fear of homosexuality, when he met a man who wanted to publish a book of his poetry, but really wanted him, as did Bruce. But this time, rather than fleeing, he talked with Bruce about it. The latter listened to his conflict and confusion and said that Hugh did not need to break a friendship just because he did not like a homosexual relationship. That one could like a man and be close to him without necessarily getting homosexually involved was a revelation. Bruce also pointed out that Hugh rarely put himself in the place of others and empathized with their feelings. These remarks reminded him of comments that Gregory had made along the same line. All these experiences helped him "start being decent toward people."

One could question if a shift in his personality occurred this simply; nonetheless, it was an event that Hugh regarded as important, and he did have a feeling that he was starting to change. At his age, when many people are in flux, it is possible that certain experiences may have a decisive effect on their development. We are more inclined to regard the incident with Bruce as a paradigm of what was unfolding in his personality, a process that had begun with his turmoil at Harvard and represented a subtle but important shift away from his strong egocentrism.

The rest of his year away was a jumble of activity. He met a European girl who fell in love with him, or so he thought, and who followed him from one country to another. As in his previous relationships, however, he was not yet ready for close emotional ties with a woman, and the romance came to nothing. He returned to the United States and took various kinds of jobs until he could start in at Harvard again. Apparently he never had doubted that he would come back to finish his college career, and had been indecisive only as to when it would be.

The final confrontation occurred during this interim period, after he had come back home and once again was in close interaction with his father. He described it thus: "During the summer, an evil symptom developed, mainly that my affection for my father began to deteriorate . . . and then I started feeling sorry for him, because he'd get all these projects and they never came off, and he'd just go from one project to another with very sanguine hopes. He has a way of sliding off the peak of one project to another one without ever having a big breakdown."

Hugh wrestled with this "evil sympton" and his awareness of his father's shortcomings by resorting to an earlier adaptational maneuver, that of finding a substitute family during the summer. It was a family he had known for some time, and he tried to find in that circle of people the qualities he felt were lacking in his own parents. His efforts were not entirely successful, because he could not be a regular sibling and his relationships with the daughters had sexual overtones that upset the mother. He had little insight into what was going on and projected onto the mother a number of feelings of nurturance and understanding that he did not find in his own mother. The substitute family was no longer an appropriate response, however, because it kept him from confronting and working on the real issue—his own identity in comparison with his parents. He regressed in his adaptational techniques, but only temporarily.

When he returned to Harvard, he still did not know what he wanted to do with his life, but at least he felt that the interlude had been worthwhile: "I would always say to anyone: before you do anything, go to Europe and live a different kind of life entirely and meet a different kind of people, and you'll find out things about yourself you never suspected, and about the world."

The Upperclassman Years: An Increase in Insight

The amount of material in Post's interviews after he returned to Harvard was immense. Not only did he talk fast, so that the word count was high, but he interspersed his descriptive comments with opinions on a great variety of topics. He did not take part in formal extracurricular activities, but he carried on a number of projects of his own and always had ideas of things he would like to do. In this respect he seemed to reflect his father's restless interests and enthusiasm, although he never drew that conclusion himself. All of this makes our task here doubly difficult because we have to present the main outline of what was transpiring in his life without omitting important details or doing injustice to him as a person.

During his absence, Hugh had kept in touch with his freshman roommate, Gregory, and when he returned to Harvard he and Gregory became friends again. Hugh seemed as interested in this turn of events as we did, remembering some of his bitter feelings during freshman year. He recalled that previously he had taken Gregory's jokes as a sign of unfriendliness and had resented Gregory's popularity with other students. He described how his own feelings interfered by saying: "I was in such a frenzy of thinking him wrong that I couldn't stop to think how we two related as people in a room." Some of the strength of this reaction can be ascertained from his comments that he had a kind of "paranoia" that Gregory's friendliness was a trick and that really he was trying to make a fool of him. "Everything he did I viewed as an assault upon my own sense of importance and sovereignty and self-command."

Although they now lived in different Houses, Hugh and Gregory spent time together, over occasional meals, talking in each other's rooms, or on trips they made, for Hugh still had some of his wanderlust and was often able to talk Gregory into coming along. The friendship continued during the years they were both at Harvard and even after Gregory graduated. Hugh was always a bit in awe of him, feeling that Gregory's intellectual ability was better than his own, impressed by his ease with people, and a little overwhelmed by his energy. On one of their trips, time dragged for Hugh and he felt the days were incredibly long, but Gregory was busy all the time and hardly ever slept. He seemed to enjoy the trip more than Hugh.

From hindsight in viewing Hugh's college years, it is clear that his friendship with Gregory was a pivotal experience, and the fact that he could understand the defensive quality of some of his early behavior toward Gregory was an indication of his adaptive capacity. He identified with many of Gregory's personality characteristics, and even though Gregory was more conservative, Hugh admired what he stood for and began to incorporate some of Gregory's world view into his own value system. Perhaps we should not be too surprised at this experience, for Post was at an age when many people are influenced strongly by the peer group. In most of these cases, however, there have been close peer relationships in earlier years, which have crystallized in late adolescence. In Hugh's case, he had no close chums, and the origins of his capacity to relate probably resided in relationships with older persons. His grandparents and his substitute families come to mind. His idealization of a peer may have rested on his experience in indealizing these older people.

The identification with Gregory may also have been aided by the fact that there was a hint of reserve in the relationship, a certain formal quality that led them to analyze together how and why they got along rather than accepting the fact that they were good friends. Given the initial differences between the two, Hugh might well have rejected Gregory and that would have been that, but he needed friendship, and in the long run he changed enough so that he could be friendlier and used the relationship in his own growth.

Accompanying his renewed friendship with Gregory was the development of a small group of friends from both Harvard and Radcliffe with whom he felt quite comfortable and noncompetitive. He liked the roommate who had been assigned to him on his return and reported that they spent many evenings in the room together, listening to music, studying, or doing individual projects. Hugh went home for Thanksgiving vacation with him and found the members of his family exciting and charming people. In all this description there was no hint of the "paranoia" that entered into his earlier relationship with Gregory.

Hugh also pursued a friendship with a student he had known in his high school days, a man he had always liked and with whom he could now share his feelings and not feel there was a formal quality about the relationship. Hugh could be critical of him and state that he was not sufficiently open to experience, that he was too conventional, but he enjoyed him anyway. He also spent time with a Radcliffe student he had met in freshman year and with another woman friend of hers. Both relationships continued to have a curious quality that characterized most of Hugh's relationships with women; that is, Hugh tended to "worship from afar" or to have a kind of joking relationship. He would report that he was madly in love with one of them, then reveal that she was going with another man, that he was more of a confidante than a lover. He was not physically intimate with either woman, nor was there an indication that his feeling of love was reciprocated. He was, however, able to relate to them without being critical or denigrating toward them.

Such was not true in his relationship with Phyllis, which continued in an on-and-off manner, affected in part by what Gregory called his "carnal interests" and in part by his feeling that she was not sufficiently intelligent. He often wished that she would "just vanish like a snowflake." Yet he could not bring himself to break off the affair completely; he said that he had nothing to fall back on if he let her go and he felt he never would find another person who was as devoted to him. His ambivalence and unwillingness to commit himself led eventually to an incident after his junior year that became another emotional confrontation. Following one of their break-ups, she started dating another man and even thought seriously of marrying him. Hugh also was interested in another girl who lived near his home, but when he heard about the impending engagement, he talked Phyllis out of it, only to find himself then in a delicate triangle with two women. When the dust settled, he said that he had been a cad, even though his initial impulse had been to blame Phyllis, and he concluded that she still had "noble sentiments," even though he did not. The whole tenor of this conversation in the interview suggested that it was an eye-opening experience for him, especially since he then proceeded to talk about relationships he had had with other women, saying that with each one, as soon as he "had her" he began to lose interest. He went on to say that one can theorize about moral responsibility but the fact is that one is bound to have some guilt that cannot be rationalized away by saying there was no way to tell what the effect might be.

Hugh did not resolve the "Phyllis situation" while he was at Harvard, because he had not developed a sense of identity strong enough to enable him to move on to the capacity for intimacy. His self-absorption was still sufficiently high to interfere with his capacity to commit himself to a lasting relationship with a woman. He had made less progress toward intimacy than Jellinec or Kramer, who by graduation had found marriage partners, and less even than George Parker. Though the latter was not yet ready for commitment by graduation, he could enter into significant emotional interchange with the opposite sex.

The theme of moral concern noted above is an interesting one that had numerous twists and turns throughout our interviews. In his freshman year, he said quite explicitly at one point that he had no respect for authority and for rules: "Regulations I view with utter, with classic indifference. But on the other hand I'm very cautious. If I think there's much chance of my getting caught, I won't do something." His caustic comments about authority reinforced this attitude of disdain, but his caution seemed to be sufficient restraint to keep him from disciplinary trouble. His reaction to regulations on the one hand was comparable to a child's fear that he will be discovered in wrongdoing and punished. Yet, on the other hand, his behavior indicated that he had internalized some dictates, even though he was reluctant to admit them. In his freshman year, however, there seemed little to indicate that he had gone beyond these earlier stages to the conscious utilization of ethical principles as a form of control.

His reaction to the triangle with Phyllis indicated that after his return to Harvard he had begun to consider, or even accept, some guiding ethical principles other than practicality. He commented that he was influenced by the more conservative moral position taken by his friend Gregory, and said: "I always get a sort of uncomfortable feeling that in the end I'm going to make much more of Gregory's view of life than Gregory." His friend had helped him begin grasping the difference between being civilized and being impulsive. "Gregory hankers after an artistic world in which love can last, heroism is possible, action can be taken to some effect, and in which life is something which proceeds from one point to another with perceptible continuity rather than merely drifting around. I'm beginning to feel much the say way."

These words may have represented one of Hugh's more poetic moments, but nothing like this appeared in his freshman year. When he was a senior, he said: "I don't believe in God but I've got a conscience." Whether the change was due to a surfacing of sentiments earlier suppressed or to the development of a new pattern was not clear in his interviews. We suspect that his new world view may have had its origin in his grandparent's behavior and philosophy, but from whatever source, the ideas had now become internalized.

One of the most important themes in Hugh Post's story concerns his creative efforts in writing. When he returned to Harvard from his leave, he announced that he had been working on a novel. This in itself was not new. Since middle adolescence he had been writing, but he said that it was the first time he had attempted to construct a story about people other than himself. Still he seemed dissatisfied, because he filed it away without reading it. In his sophomore year, musing about the writing, he said that the big trouble was in himself, that he was not yet old enough to write well. He could write good paragraphs, and pages, and even chapters, but the whole "was always a mess." He felt embarrassed by emotions and could not yet carry a theme throughout a book, but would tend to undercut it as he went along. These comments struck us as most perceptive on his part, especially for someone who in the past had been so obtuse about interpersonal relationships and personal motivation, and probably indicated a continued openness for growth.

Hugh put his writing aside, not to pick it up again until he was a senior. At that time he wrote an honors thesis, and when it was finished he threw himself once again into doing a novel. It was not completed by the time he had graduated, but he liked it and said that for the first time he had done something he thought could stand by itself. His plot concerned the relationship between a father and son, and a girl, and the manner in which the son handled his disillusionment with the other two characters. The son comes to understand the human frailty of the others and the effect of loneliness and trauma on their subsequent actions and to use that understanding in shaping some of his own decisions. In talking about the theme of disillusionment, Hugh said: "It's more oneself one is finding out something about, . . . one is discovering something about one's own illusions, rather than finding out about the real state of the world." We assumed that there was an autobiographical aspect to the novel, that the hero was modeled on his own experience, and that the story reflected his growing ability to accept people for what they are and to feel warmth toward them in spite of their weaknesses.

Of course, Post was not a completely changed man. His self-interest and self-absorption were still strong components in his personality. We did note during his years at Harvard a shift toward greater understanding and acceptance of other people and their behavior; we also noted some working through of his feelings about his father.

Hugh left Harvard with some sense of insecurity because he did not have definite plans for the future. He felt "insubstantial" when he compared his future goals with those of his friends. Like Kramer, he did not feel that he had ever been a part of Harvard. Even though he disavowed the importance of his college education, he did say: "I do think that I have developed a certain amount of respect for the importance of history." One certainly wonders if he was talking about history in general or his own.

Personality Development and Reorganization

There were some definitive changes in Hugh Post during the time that we knew him, changes that represented a reorganization in certain aspects of his personality. We can be more specific about these changes by considering in turn the six variables that we have followed through this book.

In the first year, Hugh held himself aloof from his social environment. Two factors contributed to this: anxiety about intimacy and preoccupation with competition. We inferred that both problems related to a fear that he might lose control of his impulses in relations with others. He turned inward upon himself and was involved with his own interests, wishes, and fears. In the five years that we knew him, his egocentrism provoked a number of confrontations; subsequently he became more aware of the feelings of others and of his effect on them. By senior year he could relate easily and constructively to his thesis advisor, he could sympathize with his father's shortcomings and feel less competitive with him, he could consider the reciprocal factors in his relationships with women, and he could be more concerned with politics and the world scene. By senior year he was still introverted, but he had turned outward sufficiently to become better liked and more effective in interpersonal relations.

Post probably changed more in *object relations* than many of our other cases, but his self-absorption or narcissism was also greater in the beginning, and thus he had farther to go in development. Our tests reflected this change. His score on the social scale of the Allport-Vernon-Lindzey Scale of Values increased considerably; he also increased in both inclusion scales of the FIRO. One of the more striking changes was on the Rorschach, where he shifted from giving CF responses—that is, color responses with little form content—to FC responses—that is, color responses where form is dominant. In commenting on this change and on his general Rorschach pattern,

Dr. McArthur said: "He must be showing some improvement in interpersonal relations. Still an introvert, he may nonetheless by now have become smoother with people."

Concurrently, his *self-esteem* increased and was more stable by senior year. His manner in the interviews was more relaxed and self-confident, and he spoke of a greater sense of integration, of things "fitting together" within himself. Our test results reflected this change. In his freshman year his score on the self-acceptance scale was much below the mean for the whole sample; in senior year it reached the class mean, which also in the interval had increased. Of most interest, however, were his responses to the "Who Am I?" test. In freshman year the first part of the test consisted of responses that defined his place in his family and at Harvard, so-called *consensual* responses. Toward the end of the test, he listed such things as "the one who was expelled from class, the one who has no money, a person with an inferiority complex, a bit of matter, a genius with no talent, and nobody." His final response to the question, "who am I?" was "I don't know." Practically none of these negative self-references were given in the senior year; rather his responses had an adventuresome, wide-ranging quality to them that implied a certain enthusiasm for life. The only questionable referent was his combination of the last two responses into "Jack of all trades, master of none."

In comparison with the other cases that we have presented, Hugh's self-esteem was unusually low when he matriculated, and by senior year was not markedly different from the others. But the important aspect of the change was not in comparison to other students, but in considering the effect on him of moving from low to moderate self-regard. That effect was considerable.

In contrast, Post's *interests* did not change much; what change did occur was in the strengthening of certain patterns, not in a shifting. On the Strong Vocational Interest Blank, in the freshman year he was high on occupations that demand verbal facility and creativity, and also on natural science scales, occupations such as author, artist, architect, musician, mathematician, and physicist. His scores on occupations in the social service grouping were very low. In the senior year, his scores on verbal and creative occupations were still high and scores on helping occupations were still low. There was an increase in natural science scales to a prominent place in his interest profile. Almost all of his high scores were in occupations that are individually oriented or involve working with things, and few involved a close working with people.

By senior year there was some clarification in *goal-directed behavior* and the development of a value position on which goal-directed activity could be based. He was more inclined to want to do well on something for its own sake or for his own satisfaction rather than in the interests of competition with others. His view of the world was somewhat more traditional in that he was more inclined to emphasize action and control of the environment for man's benefit. He was inclined to view himself as able to do something within that kind of a world, but what he would do was still open and diffuse. We might say that goal possibilities were more realistically oriented by senior year but still somewhat vague. To this extent, he shared something in common with Jonathan Thackery, but he did not have the fantasies of being a bum that entered Jonathan's thoughts about the future. Both were unsure where they would go, but Hugh had a firmer idea that he could and would do something. He had a greater sense of continuity with his past, a greater feeling that he was a certain kind of person, and showed a greater willingness to be directed in his actions by dictates of conscience than he had had when he entered.

Changes in *mood* were subtle but interesting. Although there was some depression in his first year at Harvard, he could not talk about it openly as Kramer or Jellinec did. There seemed to be a sense of emptiness he could not articulate, and he handled it by being very active, both in speech and in his daily round of activities. By senior year this had altered to a more generally happy tone. He felt less empty and felt less need for constant activity. For Post, however, mood and mood swings were less prominent in our assessment than for Kramer or Jellinec.

When we turn to the various aspects of *control*, once again we find some important changes. In his freshman year, Hugh was not closely in touch with his impulses and did not feel marked anxiety, because he warded these things off through intellectualization, projection, and denial. His anger came out in sarcasm and at times was projected into the idea that people were making fun of him or making a fool of him. He would not let himself get close to people, because, we think, he was afraid they would re-

ject him. The freshman Rorschach protocol indicated that his
defenses were necessary to hold in check a potentiality for impulsive behavior. Hugh must have been aware of this, perhaps subcon-
sciously, and kept himself removed from trouble. By senior year
he felt more in control, more tolerant of his anxiety, and thus felt
more confortable in expressing his feelings and in loosening some
of his defenses. He did not need to use projection or denial as much.
He still was not comfortable with impulse control, but, as Dr. Mc-
Arthur said in his senior Rorschach report, "Our prognosis would
be that Post is going to form an adult character structure out of
his borderline neurotic style."

In the directing of energy, Post had a unique cognitive style that
involved verbal fluency. He talked rapidly in the interviews and
covered a great range of topics. He taxed the examiner on the
Rorschach with the number and speed of his responses. He was verb-
ally facile, even though not conceptually deep. On one course
examination in the freshman year, the grader wrote, "You overwhelm the reader with your erudition," to which Hugh responded
to us, "All I did was to quote some Latin." He had a quiz-kid style,
which helped him get good grades and brought favorable responses
from teachers. Also, he had substantial energy and could carry extra
courses and outside activities without feeling burdened. He was an
active person. But in the freshman year his activities were somewhat
helter-skelter and not part of a life plan, as we might expect from
what we know about his goal-directed behavior.

By senior year Post was doing fewer things but using his intellectual resources more effectively. His cognitive style still had a multi-
ple-choice quality, his creativity still had both real and specious
qualities (to quote McArthur's impressions from his Rorschach),
and there were still deficiencies in intellectual discipline. But by
graduation he showed signs of ability to form ideas with utilitarian
consequences and to do concrete intellectual chores. In short, there
was a change toward greater intellectual control and more effective
utilization of energy. He was still immature in this regard, but he
had made significant progress.

When we first knew Hugh Post, his principle procedures in handling painful affect, or his techniques for management of tension,
were to be abrasive and to hold people off or to leave the situation.
His year of travel was in the service of that latter procedure, and

for him it was a helpful event. By senior year he was better able to handle painful situations by talking them out, as he had first learned to do with Bruce in Rome. He could not use this approach with everybody, particularly with women, and still continued the use of flight as a way of reducing pain. Once again, however, he had made progress toward more effective coping procedures.

We cannot leave this case without some speculation about the effect of Harvard on him. He says that there was little, or less than in most of our other cases. He may have been right. If he had gone elsewhere, he would have needed a college with intellectual challenge and with personal freedom, because these two qualities were important to him at Harvard. He needed the former to test himself and discover that he was capable. With that knowledge, he could be less frantic about his competitiveness. He needed freedom to use his own particular coping mechanisms and to do with people as he pleased. A college that made interpersonal or institutional demands on him would have been sufficiently threatening so that he might not have returned. Harvard probably helped him most by letting him be himself, by acceding to his idiosyncrasies, and by giving him intellectual stimulation at the times and at the pace that he desired.

Chapter 9 / Change and Continuity

The five young men whose lives we shared in the preceding chapters were chosen for presentation because each in his own particular way illustrated some of the processes that we have identified as constituting personal growth in college. Five cases cannot encompass the complexity of development, but they can convey the main lines of our thinking and conclusions. They also show how we used the clinical method to understand the dynamic process in our subjects, and how we made generalizations about change and personality growth from our naturalistic observations. These people were not representative of our total sample in any statistical manner, but they do exemplify the kinds of growth processes that we observed in many other students.

The personality change in our five cases, with the possible exception of Hugh Post, was quiet, subtle, and not very exciting. It was evolutionary change, more difficult to describe than change that is dramatic, abrupt, and revolutionary. As we have noted, the majority of our subjects did not show behavior that we could classify as crisis.

The type of change we have documented has not been commonly reported in the psychological literature, although some studies in the last decade have reported data of the same kind.[1] The impor-

1. For personality development among high school students, the reader is referred to Daniel Offer, *The Psychological World of the Teen-Ager* (New York:

tance of our account of evolutionary change and continuity as a conceptual model of development lies in the possibility it offers for a better balance in psychological theories about development in adolescence and early adulthood, leading to less emphasis on turmoil and disruption as the expected pattern. As we noted in Chapter 2, the understanding of these years has been heavily influenced by data from the consulting room, and our information from people without symptoms of emotional disturbance may have a compensatory effect on theoretical formulations. Furthermore, there may be a better understanding of illness and methods of crisis intervention because knowledge about mechanisms of coping and the development of adaptive capacity can provide a gauge for assessing the degree of illness and the potential in a patient for more effective behavior. The effect of data from the consulting room has been to emphasize the defensive aspects of ego-functioning, whereas material like that in our report highlights the coping aspects of the ego.

Subsequent to our research, there has been a striking alteration in the overt life style and activity of students in many American colleges and of young adults who are not attending college. As a consequence, one might wonder whether our conclusions would have been different had our study taken place five years later. Might we have put more emphasis on the occurrence of crisis? Might we have seen more dramatic or sensational change? Certainly, there was nothing outstanding in our data on which we could predict the subsequent life-style alterations, and even in retrospect the interviews and tests give no clear hints of what was to come. To be sure, we did not probe for precursors of the present social behavior patterns, because we did not expect them, and thus we may have missed some of the earliest signs. The question of the meaning of this new behavior for an understanding of personality development in adolescence and early adulthood cannot be truly answered without new data. Our recent experience with Harvard students, however, in a nonresearch capacity, makes us think that the contrast between our subjects and students of the present day is one primarily of form or content, not process. We have the impression that the majority of students

Basic Books, 1969). For studies concerning college students, see Joseph Katz and Associates, *No Time for Youth* (San Francisco: Jossey-Bass, 1968), and Douglas H. Heath, *Explorations of Maturity* (New York: Appleton-Century-Crofts, 1965).

today are facing the same developmental issues and handling them without crisis, as did our students, and that evolutionary change using continuity is more common than revolutionary change.

We do not mean to minimize the effect on personality functioning of environmental pressures and the stress-inducing quality of the social change taking place in our society. Some students today are undoubtedly reacting with greater emotional disruption in their lives than they would in times of social stability. But we are not yet impressed with a real difference in development and the necessity of revising theory. Subsequent research and the passage of time will be the judges of that opinion.

With these introductory remarks in mind, it is appropriate to summarize in general terms our conclusions about adaptation and change and then turn to more specific material on the six variables. In Chapter 2 we stated that the most comprehensive characterization of what happened to our students was a growth in adaptive capacity. We defined adaptation as coping reasonably and advantageously with the environment and achieving a mutual transformation of both the person and his environment. We found that some people were more adept at achieving a mutual transformation than others and that there was change in coping ability over the four years of college. We have used the term *adaptive capacity,* and have noted the possibility of growth in adaptive capacity through time.

The primary change in adaptation between freshman and senior year for the great majority of our students consisted of better evaluation of the student's own skills and emotional resources and more effective assessment of the pressures or expectations from the environment. As to the first of these, most students modified their behavior through greater insight into their own personality functioning and a greater awareness of areas where environmental pressures might upset them. The insight helped them integrate more fully the various components of personality functioning, such as attitudes, goals, needs, and coping and defense mechanisms. By an increase in self-understanding, many students appeared to be more flexible in the range of responses they could offer to new situations and less involved in self-centered concerns. This modification and integration of personal factors produced a greater efficiency of personality functioning and is what we have referred to in earlier chapters as *autoplastic* change.

At the same time, our students learned to deal with the environment in more constructive terms. Their assessment of other people and events was improved in part because of cognitive factors; that is, they had more facts with which to work and were more experienced in experimental thinking. They became more aware of the areas where they had an option to accept or reject demands from the environment. One of the more important changes over the four years was the increase in feeling of personal power in dealing with people and things and thus a greater sense of being able to alter the environment or at least to be less at its mercy. Many students were able to incorporate this feeling of control into their occupational and social goals. Part of the change was in being more comfortable in exercising control over others where such control was necessary and appropriate, and that comfort in turn was based on a greater feeling of security with others, both adults and peers. This modification in relating to people and responding to events led to more effective social behavior and describes what we referred to in earlier chapters as *alloplastic* change.

Our conclusions about growth in adaptive capacity are based on observations of adaptation primarily to one environment, that of Harvard College. Although the specific qualities of that environment have not been spelled out here in detail, reference has been made to the high academic expectations and to the emphasis on privacy and freedom of choice.[2] The flexibility of environmental demands was probably greater than might have been found in some other colleges, in the military services, or in many jobs. We cannot be certain that success in adapting to Harvard would be predictive of success in adapting to other environments, especially more limiting ones, and we have no certain ways of putting probability limits around our statements about adaptive capacity. It is a reasonable hypothesis that behavior at Harvard will be associated with similar

2. The sociologists on the project staff, Dr. Charles E. Bidwell and Dr. Rebecca S. Vreeland, studied the departmental and residential aspects of Harvard, using interviews with faculty members and analyzing public documents. The reader will find in their book a fuller explanation of the social pressures and values in the Harvard environment. See Charles E. Bidwell and Rebecca S. Vreeland, *College Organization and Student Change* (Chicago: University of Chicago Press, in press).

behavior in other environments, but data from the future of our subjects will be necessary to confirm or reject that hypothesis.

Temporal Qualities of Change

The next task is to return to the crisis and continuity models of growth discussed in Chapter 2 and to apply them to the five cases that have been presented. Four major patterns can be described, patterns that combine a judgment about the level of development and about the role of crisis or continuity in attaining that level.

Progressive Maturation

The predominant feature of this pattern was a sense of steady growth and a strong feeling of continuity between past and present experiences. The first three cases fall into this pattern, and it was the one most characteristic of our sample of students. This does not mean that there were no periods of turmoil or crisis, because both Jellinec and Kramer felt quite anxious or depressed at times during their four years at Harvard. But in these periods they were able to interact effectively with the environment in spite of the crisis and to find ways of working out of the crisis. Kramer could confront his depression and realize that he needed to remove himself from Harvard for short periods; in that way he could keep from being overwhelmed.

To summarize and underscore comments made in the case presentations, continuity was important for our students because they could utilize *styles of coping* that had been effective for them in the past. This was partly due to the presence of superior motor and cognitive skills, as in Jellinec's athletic prowess and the others' academic accomplishments, but it was the manner in which skills were used that was important. Jellinec was a team man who enjoyed winning but who also contributed to the spirit of camaraderie, of team spirit, and leadership. He could interact with teammates in pursuit of a goal, and this adaptive technique was useful in coping with prep school and college. Also, the experience of emotional sharing in his large family, especially with older people, could be brought into the college years, and, for example, made his relationship with his senior tutor a personally fulfilling as well as an intellectually rewarding experience. Although Parker's penchant for fun and games, which went back into the permissive aspects of his family circle, would be thought by some to be counterproductive in an academically demanding college, it served him well at Harvard. It led him into interactions in which he could discharge tension, but in which he could also find companionship and even deep friendship, factors more important to his development than high grades.

Continuity was also important because students could utilize *previous identifications,* with parents, and with father in particular, but also with other adults and with siblings. Admired qualities of these identification figures were incorporated in the student's own personality. College provided the cognitive and emotional distance from these people that was necessary for the sifting out of feelings about parents and others and the acceptance of their qualities in oneself. We cited the cases of Kramer and Parker as the best examples of this point. From freshman year, both were aware of characteristics in their fathers that had made them successful in occupation and community, but it took the son until senior year to realize how much he had in common with his father. Jellinec had a different situation, and it was with the nurturant qualities of his mother and the competitive factors in his older brothers that he had to come to terms. In retrospect, stable and admired identification figures were important in the psychological development of the majority of our students.

Delayed Maturation

A small number of students seemed to be more confused about themselves and the future when they graduated from college than when they entered. In part, this was related to the fact that they sensed a discontinuity with the past that was heightened by the college experience, and they had difficulty in developing new and different patterns of behavior. They were not able in the four years to evolve a meaningful set of value orientations, to decide on an occupational direction, or to develop certainty about their strengths and weaknesses. They remained unsure about their negotiable talents.

The discontinuity was of two kinds: between the student and

the personality characteristics of his parents and between the student and his cultural background. These two, of course, are not unrelated. Jonathan Thackery is a good illustration of this pattern. He found little in common with his father's occupation or with his parents' style of life and the things that were important to them. Their life centered on church activities, on the comings and goings of family and friends, and had little place for literature or the world outside. This was too constraining for Jonathan. When he applied to Harvard, he recognized the lack of common interests with them, and this feeling was accentuated by his experiences as an undergraduate. But he had not found by graduation a coherent scheme of life to replace the kind he had left at home, and we anticipated that he would search for some time before settling on one.

A sense of discontinuity did not come about in all cases where there was a contrast between a student's background and his experience at college. Jellinec, for example, had come a great distance culturally when he arrived at Harvard. His boyhood experiences and the culture of the Great Plains were not comparable to the urban sophistication of Cambridge. Yet he felt tied to that background, felt he could accept and utilize the constructive aspects of it, in a way that Thackery did not. Some of our Black students came from city ghettos or the rural South, and for them the transition to Harvard was akin to culture shock. But they came to Harvard at a moment in history when a sense of racial identification was strong, and they felt a keen sense of continuity with their cultural background and often with family members.

The sense of discontinuity appeared primarily in students who, in addition to feeling the cultural gap, also lacked solid identifications, either with particular individuals or with an ethnic or religious group. Again we can cite Thackery, who could identify but little with either mother or father and who mentioned no other adults in his school years with whom he had any sustained emotional involvement. His grandfather was an important person in his earliest years, but that relationship did not extend sufficiently into his later development. Thackery had no solid roots in individual people, and also he had no identification with a larger social group, as did the Black students.

The confusion and indecision of students who represented a delay in maturation was not behavior that we viewed as evidence of crisis.

At times they were unhappy and depressed, at times tense and anxious. They did not adapt as successfully as our first three cases, because they seemed more at the mercy of their environment, less able to engage and transform it. They adjusted but did not adapt. Their behavior had more of the quality of searching and of waiting than it did of disruption. Because there was a delay in development, we wondered about the future; might a crisis be necessary before significant growth took place? That is a real possibility, but we had no evidence to support our speculation.

Crisis and Reintegration

Some students presented a more classic picture of late adolescent disturbance, of the kind that often appears in the consulting room and has contributed a good deal to the picture of adolescence and young adulthood as a time of turmoil. Hugh Post was an example. He did not seek professional help for his problem and would probably have resisted the suggestion for such a move; instead, he chose to leave the scene of the crisis to try and work things out. When he left Harvard, he was angry and confused, but he was also more frightened than he could admit to us or perhaps even to himself. His customary coping mechanisms were not able to help him contain his anxiety to the point of adjusting, much less of adapting.

There were other students, although still constituting a minority of our sample, who underwent a fairly severe crisis in college. One student came to us in his junior year, apart from the research interviews, to seek some help because he was so anxious that he could not sleep or study effectively. He was disturbed about an interpersonal situation that made him feel second-rate, and this accentuated a generalized feeling of insecurity and inferiority that went back to his mother's death in early adolescence. We made a referral for therapy, but he could not accept such a move at the time and limped through his senior year with a poor academic record and insufficient credits to graduate. Only then could he accept professional help and work out a delayed grief reaction.

There were many reasons for the onset of a crisis when one compared particular cases, but some broad generalizations can be made about the pattern. These students came to college with certain deficiencies in their experiences with adaptation and certain limitations in the effectiveness of their coping mechanisms. Hugh Post had not learned how to share experiences with peers and did not know how to give of himself in an emotional sense as well as to take. During his years of latency and adolescence, he had few friends and participated in few activities that involved cooperation and mutual interchange. His insecurity about interpersonal relationships led him to be sarcastic and openly critical of others and to withdraw into activities that were solitary in nature.

The other student, whom we described briefly above, was the son of a famous father and did not have intellectual or personal skills equal to his father's; or at least he did not think so. When his mother died, a strong source of his security was cut off and he could not share his feelings of grief, guilt, and anger with his father or siblings. His situation was different from that experienced by Jellinec, because the latter had a full grief reaction, shared quite openly with his older brothers and sisters, and he had little residue of anger or guilt.

Students who were vulnerable to crisis also had problems with early identification figures and had considerable hostility toward male figures, particularly their fathers. The problem was not the same as in our previous pattern, where there was a cultural or personal gap; rather it was in the nature of an interference, where the student could not accept qualities of adults who were in parental or other roles of control. Hugh Post, in his early interviews, often downgraded his father because he could not keep an idea or plan going for a long time, because he could not control his expenditure of money, and because he was more interested in his own activities than in those of his family. In his early years Post had felt a certain sense of abandonment when he had to live with his grandparents for months at a time, and he blamed his father for this. He had few positive things to say about either parent, reserving such comments primarily for his grandparents, who, unfortunately, had become difficult and senile in the later years. After Post came back to Harvard, however, and was reintegrating elements in his personality, he began to view his father in a much more human way, to tolerate his weaknesses and to find qualities in his personality that had merit.

For people in this pattern of crisis and reintegration, the sense of continuity was impaired or interfered with by negative feelings, and the self was viewed as inferior and vulnerable. They felt over-whelmed when the crisis came on and they could no longer cope effectively, and resolution of the crisis involved coming to terms with their feelings of guilt and anger and helplessness. Once that confrontation took place, they could then begin to use elements of past relationships and earlier patterns of behavior in new ways.

Deterioration

We had a very few pathological cases in our sample, where the development not only slowed but actually regressed and serious disturbances in cognitive and emotional functioning took place. One student gave us concern in his freshman interviews because his statements about his ability and his relationships with other people did not fit with what we sensed in his behavior. There was a grandiose quality to his feelings about himself that struck us as involving a certain amount of delusion. He could not evalu-ate his effect on other people in a realistic sense and was quite distraught when he was rejected rather than accepted by others. The Rorschach test also had signs that suggested an incipient psychotic process, signs that McArthur liked to call "the lush Brazilian jungle of fantasy." His capacity for reality-testing on the Rorschach was also impaired. Yet he continued in his freshman year to function satisfactorily in the academic realm and received mostly honor grades. He was an extremely bright young man. In his sophomore year he began to express some concerns about his sexual adjustment and seemed very anxious about homosexuality. But he could not seem to face his problems directly and inter-posed in the discussion of problems his unrealistic fantasies about his ability and his future attainments. He left Harvard in the middle of that year, ostensibly to travel and to write, but he was also having difficulty in concentrating on his studies and his academic record was much below his freshman year.

Subsequently, he sought some help from two of the more uncon-ventional schools of psychotherapy, but in neither case did he com-mit himself to the treatment for more than two months. He returned to Cambridge with the thought of enrolling in the College again and came to see us, hoping to collect once more the small stipend that we had for research subjects. After a short interview, however, he seemed so uneasy and suspicious that we concluded, and he agreed, that it would not be wise to continue. Suggestions were offered for referral and treatment, but he was not willing to accept the help and, as there were no indications that he was a danger to himself or to others, we could not prevail upon him further.

This student was different from Hugh Post; he showed much more confusion between reality and fantasy and relied increasingly on fantasy as environmental stresses increased. The pressure to become independent, as part of the student role, and to form stable and intimate relations with other people led to a breakdown of previous coping mechanisms and a retreat or regression into more primitive defenses.

Various kinds of serious disturbances were evident in about 5 percent of our total sample of students in both of the college classes we studied, a figure comparable with that to be expected in the population as a whole.

We have noted the deterioration pattern only to round out our scheme and did not present a full case because of its infrequency in the college population. Also, psychopathological development in adolescence and young adulthood has been studied in great detail, whereas much less attention has been given to normal or nonpathological growth.

These four patterns do not exhaust the possible ways of describing the changes in personality functioning during college. Various subgroups within progressive maturation might be defined, or other major patterns might be developed. Nonetheless, the four patterns seemed to fit our data rather well, at least to our minds, and do emphasize the conceptual balance between crisis and continuity, between evolutionary and revolutionary development, that has been a consistent theme of this book.

Changes in Terms of the Six Categories

Our theoretical assumptions about personality, although eclectic, led us to focus on certain psychological variables where change occurred over the four years of college. We noted at the beginning of Chapter 4 that these variables stood out in the data, but certainly that statement should be amended to include that they stood out for us, with our particular "set" toward understanding the lives of people. We felt, as we reviewed the data from our interviews, that the changes on these variables led to a better integration of personality by graduation, which in turn led to a heightened capacity for adaptation.

In the following summary of the general changes, or lack thereof, on each variable, reference will be made from time to time to data from "paper and pencil" tests and questionnaires administered to the larger survey sample from the classes of 1964 and 1965. These data are not intended to offer validation for the conclusions drawn in this book, but are used to highlight findings derived from our use of the clinical method. This does indicate an interesting and important factor in the Harvard Student Study that has not been discussed here but appears in other publications about the research.[3] Conclusions drawn from quite different sources of information—projective tests, interviews, and "paper and pencil" tests and questionnaires—had much in common and served to enrich our most general feelings about personality change in college. A fuller description of these integrated conclusions will be presented in a future publication.

Object Relations

The students in our sample felt that they changed in their mode of relating to other people, and they valued this change. Our assessment, through the interviews, confirmed that feeling. Furthermore, various measures from the larger questionnaire study indicated statistically significant changes in both attitudes and actions toward people. Bruce Finnie[4] has referred to this in his analysis of the test and questionnaire data as the "movement toward people" factor. He found a large and steady increase in the amount of time students spent in social interaction and in dating, and his analysis gives evidence that heterosexual activity of all kinds increased. In general, students had more new friends by senior year and interacted with

3. John M. Whitely and Hazel Z. Sprandel (eds.), *The Growth and Development of College Students*, Student Personnel Series no. 12 (Washington, D.C.: American Personnel and Guidance Association, 1970).

4. Bruce Finnie, "The Statistical Assessment of Personality Change," in Whitely and Sprandel, *Growth and Development*, pp. 24–30.

them primarily through direct relationships, or what the sociologists would call informal relationships in contrast to interaction as members of formal organizations. Various measures of introversion-extroversion changed strongly toward the latter. Finally, there was an increase in the tendency to choose the personal and particular in opposition to the universal and abstract when confronted with a conflict.

We noted from our interview material that there was an increase in the depth of friendship relationships, or, to use Erikson's term, in the extent of intimacy. For most students, there was by graduation a greater ability to accept their friends and to have a constancy in the relationship that could accommodate both pleasant and unpleasant aspects of the friends' personalities. Accompanying this was a sense of reciprocity, that friends returned the feeling. Joseph Kramer implied this, as we noted previously, when he described his relationship with Rebecca: "I think she knows me. I don't feel the same impetus to enforce my desires or opinions that I do in activity here. I feel I can talk to her without putting on any pretensions." George Parker developed a similar relationship with his roommate, Todd Jackson, whom he described as "closer than a close friend."

Concurrently, relationships with parents, particularly with the father, were worked out over the course of time. Students could better differentiate between those aspects of the father's personality which they liked and wanted to manifest in their own behavior and those qualities of the father which they could not accept. This was variously expressed in ideas about style of life, occupational plans, or value orientations. George Parker, for example, developed a greater acceptance of his father's insistence on financial responsibility, could better understand and agree with his father's concerns for the community in which the Parker family lived, and, of course, settled on the same occupation as his father. Although Hugh Post had little desire to follow in his father's footsteps, he became more accepting of those qualities he had previously found annoying in his father and felt closer to him as a person.

The working out of feelings about the father seemed to be associated with change in other relationships: with the mother, for example, where there was often an improvement in understanding. We cannot be sure that working through feelings about the father was the primary alteration that caused change in perception of the mother, but we do know that our subjects talked less about the mother in the interviews. Altered relationships with parents were associated with greater freedom for intimate relationships with peers. Our subjects seemed to have disengaged sufficiently from intensity of feelings, and conflicts of feelings, about parents to commit themselves wholeheartedly to someone else. Thus, work on one life detail, relations with the father, had wide-ranging ramifications.

The developmental process seemed to be most successful when students had earlier identifications with parents or other adults that had been satisfying and that provided attitudes, values, or ways of coping that the student could adapt to his own personality. Among the cases we have presented, Jonathan Thackery had the fewest early identifications, and he was the one, also, who changed the least in object relations.

Being at college was important to these changes because of the physical separation from parents, which provided an opportunity for more objective assessment of the home and gave the student an occasion to compare his situation with others. The college environment also encouraged autonomy, and the interviews indicated that most parents expected an increase in autonomy by their offspring. Students were thus encouraged to re-evaluate the relationship between themselves and their parents and to take a stand on their own values and behaviors. The college environment further offered realistic parental surrogates in teachers or coaches with whom students could continue some of the satisfying interaction with parents without the emotional intensity that would be characteristic of parent-son interchange.

In various ways, our subjects changed their social outlook and expressed greater concern or interest in history, politics, or social movements. Even though some behavioral scientists characterized the early sixties as a time of social apathy on the part of students, we found a readiness in our subjects to turn outward and adopt a responsibility for society. This turning outward was not as explicit in the lives of the five men in this book as in others of the forty-one that were interviewed. Many of them were making serious plans for a career in politics or the foreign service or thought of professions like law or medicine as vehicles for ameliorating the condition of many of the disadvantaged in our society.

Often students had a social idealism when they matriculated but did not know how to put it into effect. College aided in providing avenues for expressing ideals, for implementing what previously might have been only wish or fantasy. College induced change by giving the student time and freedom to explore the social order, to look at it abstractly and analytically. Lectures, courses, club meetings, and bull sessions enabled students to become more sensitive to social needs and the ways in which they could utilize their skills in meeting those needs. The range of experience and points of view among students and faculty offered a stimulating environment in which to develop and test out new ideas.

It is not surprising that the social and political concern of the last few years was most evident on college campuses, and indeed that one of the primary targets for social change was often the college itself. But we did not predict the social upheaval from the changes we observed in our students on object relations. The "movement toward people" factor and the greater interest in people than in academic experience was interpreted by us as a normal developmental step toward involvement with the peer group rather than as a precursor of social concern on a scale and dimension not usually manifested among Harvard students, or American youth in general, prior to 1965. Because our emphasis was on the phase-specific psychology of maturation and less on the psychosocial approach, we did not sufficiently anticipate the concurrence of social and political changes and the association with our data.

Self-Esteem

There was a significant increase in various measures of self-esteem and self-worth for the total group of students in the project, change on such tests as the self-acceptance scale, and the self-confidence scale from the Myers Briggs Type Indicator. One reason for this change, which the interviews revealed, was an increase in the sense of competence, as Robert White[5] uses that concept. By the time of graduation, most students had decided that they were good for something and had learned the areas where their strengths lay. Some

5. Robert W. White, "Motivation Reconsidered: The Concept of Competence," *Psychological Review,* 66 (September 1959), 297–333.

students developed a sense of competence in new areas, as in the case of Jason Jellinec, who found greater assurance about his intellectual ability and confidence about holding his own with his peers in the realm of ideas as well as on the baseball diamond.

Accompanying the increased assurance about the use of skills was a greater sense of power, expressed in the ability to have an effect on people and events. Also, the realization of how the student might use his power was based by graduation more on reality factors than on the feeling of omnipotentiality that is often characteristic of the idealistic fantasies and aspirations of adolescents. Our subjects now knew what they could do, not merely what they hoped or dreamed they might do.

The Harvard environment was important in these changes because it offered a great number of diverse activities that could bring satisfaction in accomplishment and, in some cases, prestige and public acclaim. Unlike some other colleges, there are not many activities that are recognized by all students as being the most prestigious. There are no standard pathways to the "big man on campus" syndrome. Rather, the emphasis on individuality and the great range of possible activities at the College means that there are many avenues for competence. Of course, this situation contains a weakness as well as strength. The extensiveness of possibilities may offer too many exciting avenues for the very intelligent or creative individuals, especially if these people do not have definite ideas about what they want to do. This happened to Jonathan Thackery, and, in the freshman year, it happened to Hugh Post. After his time away, Post could be much more selective about how he used the environment.

One particular aspect of the academic experience also deserves special attention here: the effect on self-esteem of the senior honors thesis. Not all departments require a thesis as a portion of the evaluation for honors, nor do all students have the necessary academic average or the motivation to undertake an honors thesis where it is required. Finally, not all students who write a thesis find it a critical experience in their undergraduate careers. In spite of these exceptions, we were impressed by the gain that can accrue in some cases from the experience. It may be the first time that a student has done independent work where the standards are exacting, where he has a chance to develop and test his own ideas and then to defend them in oral examination. When that process works successfully, the student may feel not only a greater sense of power, but also a sense of colleagueship with adults. Both often lead to increased self-esteem. For Jason Jellinec, the writing of a thesis was painful, but the experience, when completed, was one of the most significant of his Harvard years. In the case of Hugh Post, we had reason to believe that writing a superior thesis helped free him from some concerns about evaluation of his writing and enabled him to start a novel.

As well as providing a sense of intellectual achievement, the senior honors thesis, through the specific topic chosen, sometimes may contribute to the settling of concerns and conflicts from earlier years. Again, we cite the experience of Jason Jellinec, who had a reawakening of feelings and questions about his ethnic group and his mother, as a result of the data-gathering interviews for his thesis. As he mulled these things over, he could see more clearly some of the factors that had shaped his character and could feel a greater sense of ego identity. Another student, not described previously, made a study of certain aspects of the practice of medicine, a topic which helped him reappraise earlier questions and doubts about medicine as a career and led him to apply to medical school. Not all senior theses have such emotional as well as intellectual involvement, but for some students a thesis can be the impetus for personal growth.

Another reason for an increase in self-esteem was the growing capacity to relate to and be accepted by others, a point already made under our discussion of object relations. Some students developed a romantic relationship with marriage in mind, like Jellinec and Kramer. Others experienced a greater intimacy and sharing of feelings with male peers, such as Post found in his discussions with Bruce and Parker found in his relationship with his roommate, Todd. The effect of these interpersonal relationships was a greater sense of self-worth.

Mood

For most of our subjects, there was a change toward stabilization of mood over the four years; that is, shifts in mood were not as extreme or as frequent. When mood shifts did occur, they were more likely to be the result of alterations in the environment than to be the effect of internal states. Sometimes environmental events concerned the student's family life, as in a divorce by his parents or a death in the family. Sometimes college activities had an effect on mood, as was commonly seen in the pressure of examinations. National events also had an impact on the mood of individual students. The most striking of these was the assassination of President Kennedy, who was a youthful ideal for many Harvard students. There was a noticeable feeling of depression and grief among most students at that time, which lasted for at least a week. Of a different nature was the crisis over Russian missles in Cuba, which in some students was associated with anxiety and in others with anger. By and large, students handled all these environmental events with only a limited alteration in mood, although any serious disruption in family relationships took more time to resolve.

Depression as a mood occurred less frequently by senior year in most of our subjects; when it did occur, they seemed to be able to recover more quickly. They became more adept at recognizing reasons for depression and at finding ways of alleviating it, usually by talking about it with a close friend. As we reread the interview material for Jellinec and Kramer, we noted a growing awareness, as they neared senior year, of precipitants within themselves that could lead to depression and also of their vulnerability to certain kinds of environmental stress. Insight into these factors resulted in greater control of mood. As a result, they also became more aware of things they could do to abort or modify the depressed feelings. There was one exception. Jonathan Thackery appeared more at the mercy of events, either within himself or in the environment, less able to control unpleasant moods, and he changed little in this regard over the four years. For him, useful insight seemed to lie in the future.

What caused the shift toward mood stabilization? To some extent, it was probably due to a kind of mellowing process that results from growing older and accumulating experience and perspective. When a person has felt certain emotions in the past, such as depression or irritableness, and realizes that these moods, though unpleasant, were not catastrophic, he is more likely to be able to work them out when they occur in the future. In addition, the hormonal and other physiologic changes that were so strong in adolescence have lessened in young adulthood, and most poeple have learned ways of handling their reactions to body image and impulses.

At the same time, there seemed to be an indirect but important effect of the college experience. An understanding of factors that cause alteration in mood and a willingness to look into one's own personality were encouraged by certain courses; Social Relations 120 (Analysis of Interpersonal Behavior), for example, pursued introspection quite openly, but many courses in the humanities also looked at psychological processes. Informal discussions among students, the traditional bull sessions, often considered personal issues like values and attitudes or reaction styles and habits. Here is an example of how intellectualization as an ego mechanism can be used adaptively instead of only serving a defensive function, as it is more commonly viewed in writings on psychopathology. The language of psychology was much a part of the college scene, and students seemed to delight in their use of psychoanalytic terms and explanations. For many students this was a new experience because in secondary school human behavior had neither been taught as a formal subject nor given as much importance.

Two of our cases illustrate these effects. In his first two years, Joseph Kramer apparently did not like to reflect on his psychological state and indeed had difficulty in doing so, but by senior year he said that he had become more introspective and had found some value in the writings of Freud. Hugh Post, as a freshman, was uncomfortable in self-analysis and criticized others; by senior year he could report that there might be some value in a student's taking Social Relations 120 and looked more positively on social relations courses in general.

Besides encouraging the stabilization of mood by introspection and intellectualization, the college experience helped many students feel that they had greater control over their own destiny. They learned that a greater number of options were open to them than perhaps they had realized before, and they knew more clearly how they could utilize their skills in attaining these options. The effect of the growing sense of control made students feel less vulnerable to pressures from the environment and less likely to slip into unpleasant moods.

A growing sense of control is a product of both individual development and opportunities in the environment, and when the latter is perceived as unduly restrictive or repressive, there may be an effect on mood. In the relatively few years since our data were collected, a good many college students have expressed frustration with a number of aspects of our society, including the quality and structure of higher education, national priorities, and the continuation of the war in Southeast Asia. Some of these young people have said they felt their options were limited by the social system, by the pressure of the military draft, or by the unresponsiveness of the government. It is difficult to know how many students feel, as a result, a sense of being trapped or of severely limited options, but a number of commentators have described a mood of malaise in the country that did not seem to be present when we made our study. It is entirely possible that interviews with college students at the present time would show more unrest, rebelliousness, overt anger, and depression than we found among our subjects. Comparative data are needed in this situation, but it is clear that changes in mood during the college years must be considered within a social context.

Interests

From any number of vantage points, the change in interests was not remarkable in terms of direction or extent. For example, Finnie[6] did a careful statistical study of freshman and senior scores on the various occupational scales of the Strong Vocational Interest Blank for the survey sample and found that correlations between the two sets of scores were high. There were no large changes in any absolute sense. Those that did occur were away from occupations that are technical, scientific, or professional in nature and towards occupations that are more concerned with relations between people. Looking more carefully at individual items and at material from other tests, Finnie concluded that there was some change in the direction of greater openness and flexibility and greater interest in interpersonal relations.

There was little evidence in the interviews for major shifts in interest patterns. We did observe some changes, however, that could be characterized as a *deepening of interests* that were already present. The interview data in general fitted White's[7] description of one of

6. Bruce Finnie, "Interests of Harvard Students as Freshmen and Seniors," paper read at the Annual Meeting of the American Psychological Association, September 1966.

7. Robert W. White, *Lives in Progress* (New York: Holt, Rinehart and Winston, 1966).

the major accomplishments of young adulthood, a process where-
by there is greater absorption by the person in his interests, not
necessarily in terms of time commitment but certainly in terms of
emotional commitment. What we observed was a growing clarification and certainty about interest areas and a greater awareness
of how particular interests fitted in with the individual's needs,
abilities, and values. Again, as in other variables, there was movement toward more discrimination and synthesis. Jellinec, for
example, became more certain that, in addition to athletics, he
wanted activities involving some kind of interaction with people.
His choice of social relations for concentration, his thesis topic,
and his summer work all provided fulfillment of his major interest
in interacting with people. Even though Jonathan Thackery was by
graduation still somewhat confused about his identity and his future
plans, he was certain that literature, as a source of enjoyment and
creation, was a major interest that followed from his aptitudes and
was congruent with his modes of relating to people as well as in
line with the things that he thought were important in the world.
For Thackery, deepening of interests may well have been one of
the crucial aspects of his Harvard experience.

The lack of marked changes in interests, especially in an environment that allows exploration and does not force commitment, that
provides an opportunity for a moratorium in the assumption of
adult roles, requires us to consider the hypothesis that basic dispo-
sitions in interest patterns are well developed by the time of college.
One of the main functions of the college experience may then be
the presentation of alternatives for the expression of interests or
the presentation of a wider range of alternatives, through both
academic and extracurricular activities, than may have been available in the student's life heretofore. Also, the college experience may
aid the sorting process in interests through the emphasis on analysis in the classroom, the encouragement of experimental thinking,
and the evaluation that takes place in the constant disucssions or
bull sessions that are so much a part of college life. The clinical
interviews indicated that the major involvement with interests, in
the ways described, took place in the sophomore and junior year
and that in senior year the focus shifted to planning for graduate
school or a job.

One of the questions of the day is whether most students have
this kind of closure by graduation or whether they feel less commit-

ted to specific areas for the expression of interests than did our students. Casual conversation with students indicates that some are delaying an occupational decision and are not committing themselves to some of the more traditional outlets for interest patterns. Data on recent Harvard graduating classes, for example, indicated a drop of about 20 percent in the number of students who planned on attending graduate school, a change from previous years that is conspicuous by its magnitude.[8] This finding would support the idea that some students today are more inclined to keep their options open and to direct their interests toward different kinds of activities than in previous years. It is difficult to judge how pervasive this change may be, inasmuch as many students, probably a majority, do have occupational plans and are certain about ways their interests can be satisfied. The very fluidity of the present situation precludes the drawing of firm conclusions about future trends.

Finally, we must consider the tendency for the group of subjects as a whole to shift toward occupational areas that involve people. This may have been due to any one or more of a number of factors. A developmental ingredient must be considered; that is, a shift toward greater interaction with people is part of the unfolding that takes place in young adulthood. There was evidence for that trend in our findings on object relations, and the same trend could have been at work in interest patterns.

Other explanatory factors involve the environment. Charles Bidwell's[9] interviews with faculty members indicated a pervasive influence in the Harvard culture toward the importance of the humanities, the classics, and the social sciences. The natural sciences have always been strongly supported and continue to be, but there seemed to be a subtle push to give them second place. This could have led students to place more importance on subjects or occupations that deal with people and less on fields where the subject matter is divested of human qualities or personality.

Also, changes in the wider culture are taking place that emphasize the quality of life, and some of the spokesmen for this position come from the natural sciences. As our study was being conducted,

8. "The Harvard College Class of 1970," Office for Graduate and Career Plans, Harvard University, December 1970 (mimeographed).
9. Bidwell and Vreeland, *College Organization and Student Change.*

a more humanitarian approach in science could be seen in some of the science courses that had a broad general appeal to the student body. The shift in interest patterns could have been an accompaniment of the curricular shift and the general social change. Had we been blessed with historical foresight, we might have been alerted to the present decline in emphasis on the scientific method and technology as compared to the humanities.

Goal-Directed Behavior

The most important overall change in goal-directed activity was characterized by a rise in the level of aspiration. Over the four years, many students became aware that they could do more, could seek higher status activities than they had originally considered. For example, the idea of participating in the honors program had not occurred to some students when they matriculated, in part because it was an aspect of college they knew little about, but also because they were not sure they were that competent. By senior year a majority of students were in the honors program and graduated with honors. Jason Jellinec illustrates that kind of change most clearly. In high school and even at Greenwood Academy, his academic accomplishments were mediocre and his goals were more concerned with physical than intellectual activity. He did not see himself as able to accomplish much in the latter area. At Harvard, Jason did not blossom quickly; rather, the first two years involved a realization that literature was exciting, that history was meaningful, and that with hard work he might learn to write reasonably well. Only in his last two years did he discover that he had ideas that were worthwhile and that he could do academic work of honors caliber. The latter was really the result of the support and tough-mindedness of his tutor. But by the end of senior year he could think seriously of graduate school and of occupations that required a high level of intelligence and skill.

The increase in aspiration level was reflected in some of the questionnaire results Finnie has reported.[10] For the sample as a whole, he noted that between freshman and senior year there was a significant increase in the selection of jobs on the basis of

10. Finnie, "Statistical Assessment of Personality Change," in Whitely and Sprandel, *Growth and Development,* pp. 24–30.

status and prestige. Also, on the "Who Am I?" test there was an interesting change, a decrease during sophomore year in concerns with achievement, followed by a steady rise on that variable in the last two years.

Another illustration comes from the interview sample, from a Black student who had been reared in a city where schooling was segregated and of poor quality. He was very intelligent and had managed to learn a great deal in spite of the inadequate educational nurturing, but he could not forget the social need at home. His goal, when he came to Harvard, was to return to his community to teach science, a field in which he had substantial skill. That goal persisted into the beginning of his junior year, when he began to doubt the value of that career as compared with the law. He saw the latter occupation as giving him greater effectiveness in matters of civil rights, he felt there was a need for Black role models in high status professions, and he also felt he would find greater intellectual challenge in the practice of law.

A second change in goals concerned life style and values and the satisfactions to be expected from family and community living. These changes were not large and could not be compared with the radicalization of many students that has happened in the last few years. Nonetheless, they may prove to be important in subsequent years.

As an illustration for these changes, we turn first to Finnie's[11] analysis of the test and questionnaire results for all the subjects. He noted a decrease in certain traditional value positions, such as church attendance and belief in a Divine God. Students moved toward the value of relativism and the basic neutrality of human nature and away from values of absolutism and the basic good or evil of human nature. Also, when confronted with a conflict, they were as seniors more likely to choose the personal and particular over the universal and abstract. This meant an increasing willingness to bend or alter abstract principles, such as honesty, in favor of one's friends. Finally, there was a sharp decrease in the tendency toward uncritical acceptance of authoritative pronouncements in social and moral areas, as reflected in large changes on the F scale.

11. Ibid.

We noted in our interviews that goals about family and community life came to center more on a life style that allowed personal freedom in moral decisions, with less acceptance of the constraints of the social order. For example, Jonathan Thackery's statement about wanting to be a bum, even though more extreme than comments by most students, reflected a desire for personal freedom, to do with his life as he wished. George Parker was more conventional, at least in the choice of the same occupation as his father's, but he wanted life outside the law practice to be his own, to allow him to choose activities without constant reference to social restraints.

These changes were subtle ones and at the time were not sufficient to suggest some of the striking changes in life goals that have emerged in students in only the last few years. None of our subjects subscribed to Timothy Leary's call to "turn on, tune in, and drop out." Some of our subjects had a political philosophy far to the left, but we saw none of the political radicalism that has marked the recent confrontations between students and educational or civil authorities. Only in retrospect do we see that a readiness to alter the traditional value and goal structure was present to some degree in our cases.

Harvard appears to have had two effects, perhaps rather obvious ones, on goal-directed activity. The intellectual demands and the elitist feeling that are characteristic of the environment led most students to raise their occupational expectations and to feel more competent about meeting a higher level of job requirements. There was subtle but pervasive pressure toward graduate school and toward the best fulfillment of one's capacities. The environment also encouraged indvidual freedom and was permissive in the areas of personal philosophy and moral positions. There was an emphasis on personal exploration, spirited interchange on matters of politics and values, and acceptance of those who were eccentric or different from the mode. For our subjects, this combination of freedom and elitism provided for the possibility of change in goals, but tended to keep the change within broadly conventional limits.

Control

Control of Impulses On this variable we found some important changes. Though they may have been small in a quantitative sense or subtle in a clinical sense, they were central to personality functioning. The change may at first seem paradoxical, because it involved both a freeing of impulse expression and the development of greater impulse control. But when one looks more carefully, the freeing can be seen as a greater understanding of impulse life in oneself, a greater acceptance of the naturalness of emotions, and more certainty about the appropriate places and way of expressing impulses. As a result, our subjects became easier with their impulse life. At the same time, they brought more rationality into the handling of impulses, and the process became more conscious and hence more selective.

In the cases we have presented, the freeing and controlling process took different turns. Jellinec from the beginning was self-analytical, but it was not until his junior year that he began to understand the extent and sources of his anger. In his senior year he found in Betty someone who made him angry at times, but who also made him feel that it was legitimate to express anger. Because of his increased tolerance for his angry reactions, he became less prone to depression and better able to dissipate the feelings and turn back to love.

As we have noted, Kramer and Post were not comfortable with introspection as freshmen and were uneasy with some of their feelings. Both were somewhat afraid of their anger and of their nurturant and affectionate feelings. Both came to the point where they could look at their emotional reactions with some objectivity and not feel overwhelmed by them. Parker, in his early college years, personified the quip, "A man with never an unexpressed feeling," but he seemed pushed or driven in his pleasure-seeking. By his senior year he was less frantic about impulse expression, because he had a little insight into the rebellious nature of his actions. Thackery, who had been inhibited, came by his senior year to some awakening of his impulses, as perhaps was illustrated by his experience with peyote, but full freeing and greater control would come after college.

Further illustration of these conclusions from interview data can be found in Finnie's statistical analysis of the total sample and in McArthur's study of Rorschach changes.[12] In the former

12. Finnie, "Statistical Assessment of Personality Change," in Whitely and

report, there was a significant increase in the impulse expression scale over the four years and in test and questionnaire items that indicated a desire for assertive action versus value-determined restraint. Finnie interpreted his results as indicating a greater readiness to respond and a greater lack of reserve. At the same time, items about uncontrolled physical aggression showed a decrease, and there was a decrease in uncontrolled restless energy and lack of restraint.

In McArthur's data, the change was in the area of color responses, from a predominance of color-dominated, or CF, responses to those dominated by form qualities, FC. This shift represented a growing rational control over impulsive response to the environment.

Directing of Energy In the third chapter we defined this variable as the directing and guiding of cognitive, emotional, and/or motor responses. It is a variable on which all our subjects had demonstrated an adeptness at the time they matriculated. In many ways, this kind of control must have weighed as a factor in the decisions of the admissions committee as they considered potential students. Our subjects had been successful in secondary school in academic achievement, many had been leaders in social organizations or other kinds of extracurricular activities, and, of course, some had been outstanding in sports. George Parker is a case in point. Through his sophomore year in high school, he had been rather casual about school work, but in that summer he realized that he would need a better record if he wished to be admitted to a good college. In his last two years he applied himself so successfully that he won numerous academic honors; in addition, he carried on a number of work activities after school hours.

Even though our subjects had shown they could direct their energies before they came to Harvard, there were changes during the undergraduate years, changes that involved both cognitive and emotional components. Among the former, the most obvious was the growing body of knowledge each student had at his disposal, which came not only from the classroom, but also from discussion with peers and adults in the community, from travel, and from ob-

Sprandel, *Growth and Development,* pp. 24–30; and Charles C. McArthur, "Rorschachs and Harvard Men," in Whitely and Sprandel, *Growth and Development,* pp. 18–23.

servation of other competent people as they dealt with the environment. The base of facts on which a student could make a decision was considerably broadened during four years in college.

In addition to the accumulation of facts, there was a change in cognitive style, in the direction of what, in Chapter 3, we called experiemental thinking. Our subjects had experience with this kind of abstract thought before they came to Harvard, but the college environment encouraged its use in academic responsibilities and in the general social life of the community. We found among our interview subjects a subtle but clear progression from an emphasis on a dualistic, or a "black-and-white" approach to intellectual problems, to an emphasis on a complex balancing of alternatives, a "thinking in greys." Our impressions reflected the conclusions William Perry had reached after careful observation, interviewing, and testing of hundreds of Harvard undergraduates.[13] As a result of this cognitive change, students could handle the environment more effectively through planning, through taking account of contingencies, and through selecting the best alternative, given certain conditions. Not all students could apply experimental thinking equally well, nor could any particular student use it all the time. They had the fallibilities we all possess, but most of them became more sophisticated about guiding their responses and controlling the world around them.

The emotional component of change on this variable was in a greater ease or comfort with the directing of energy to control the environment, associated in many ways with the freeing of impulse expression that we discussed in the previous section. Perhaps this can be understood most clearly by examples from our cases. Joseph Kramer was less driven and somewhat less compulsive about his work by graduation, and less tense about it. George Parker had less need for sleep than in the freshman year and also found it less necessary to proclaim that college was for fun and games and not for grades. Hugh Post did not have the dawn-to-dusk round of different activities that had been characteristic of his freshman year, but could be more selective in what he did and base his selection on interest and satisfaction. In these three cases, as in many others, the direct-

13. William G. Perry, Jr., *Forms of Intellectual and Ethical Development in the College Years* (New York: Holt, Rinehart and Winston, 1968).

ing of energy was more realistic and appropriate, and work and activities less often served a defensive purpose in binding anxiety.

Management of Tension In general, there was an increased tolerance for unpleasant and painful feelings as students came to the senior year. Some of them described this change as "not being so shook up" when things did not go right, meaning that feelings of anxiety or depression were not as disabling or disruptive of functioning as they had been in previous years. In some cases, students showed more signs of overt anxiety, as on test material like the manifest anxiety scale or the Rorschach test. As we looked more carefully at such cases, we concluded that this was usually not a sign of disturbance or of greater neuroticism, but reflected instead a growing acceptance of self, within which feelings of anxiety could be allowed to surface. The anxiety in these cases was not associated with rigid defenses, nor did it lead to breakdown of functioning; indeed, in many cases it served often to motivate the student to some kind of constructive action.

There were many reasons for this change, all of which we have noted in other circumstances on the previous pages. Students had found that painful affect was usually self-limited; they had an increased sense of autonomy and power and control over their own destiny that made painful affect less threatening; they felt a greater acceptance by peers on an intimate level of emotional give-and-take; some of them were more capable of introspection and self-understanding; and some of them had worked out conflicts with father and other adults that in the past had increased guilt and dependence. All of the cases we have presented changed in some degree toward an increased tolerance of unpleasant feelings, and even in the case of Jonathan Thackery there was less denial and more openness about these matters.

Without data from other samples it is difficult to know how much these changes in the three aspects of control were due to the college experience and how much to the unfolding or developmental processes in personality and the assumption of adult status. The students themselves felt that college had been important, by separating them from parents, by forcing them to make their own decisions, by providing them with a wealth of new experiences, and by enchancing their feelings of competence and self-esteem. Yet it is quite possible that the same conditions could be found in situations other than college, and only comparative research can eventually settle the speculation.

These conclusions about changes in control lead quite naturally back to one of the major points made at the beginning of this chapter and elsewhere in the book. The changes were subtle, not dramatic, and reflected an unfolding or gradual development rather than a sudden emergence of new behavior or other striking change. The data as we saw them do not fit the crisis model of growth, and there is reason to accentuate the continuity model as another important way of conceptualizing development. By now, the reader is familiar with the argument for that position as presented in these pages. A final word is in order, however, about the relationship between crisis and continuity.

Although we have differentiated between crisis and continuity, the reader may feel that the idea of continuity is obvious to any thoughtful person and that we have made too much of the differentiation. It is true that all change is not due to crisis, or all to continuity. Persons who exhibit strong continuity will at times experience crisis, especially if they are confronted with severe threat or dissonance in the external situation. On the other hand, even the person in a major personality upheaval has some degree of continuity in development. It is also true that people who have written about adolescence from the crisis point of view could find evidence of continuity in their subjects or patients.

The predominant point of view in the psychological literature, however, has been that of the crisis model, and, as we have noted, it is all too easy to regard this as the total explanation of growth and development. In so doing, a person may de-emphasize or even miss important capacities for coping and adaptation. This has important implications for psychological theory and for making predictions about behavior, either in the abstract or in individual cases. Furthermore, the expectations that one has about behavior, based on theory, can affect the behavior of another person. Teachers and parents of adolescents are ones for whom this is particularly pertinent, and their expectations are based to a large degree on what psychologists and psychiatrists tell them.

The point does not need to be stressed further. The data from our study of Harvard students has led us to see the need for conceptual balance. Even in an era in which conflict presents itself most dramatically, there are many individuals whose development is relatively free of conflict. In the study of the lives of our students, continuity was more predominant than crisis and often was the determining feature of their development.